DETROIT
BEER

DETROIT
BEER

A History of Brewing
in the Motor City

STEPHEN C. JOHNSON

AMERICAN PALATE

Published by American Palate
A Division of The History Press
Charleston, SC
www.historypress.net

Front cover skyline photo courtesy of Ken Hipp, Flickr.

First published 2016

Manufactured in the United States

ISBN 978.1.46711.972.6

Library of Congress Control Number: 2015960010

CONTENTS

FOREWORD

My passion for craft beer started in the late '80s. I was living in Boston, where a local guy by the name of Jim Koch was making a tasty Boston lager and seemed to be doing pretty well with it. Of course, at the time we had no idea he would be one of the founding fathers of the craft beer revolution—we just knew he was definitely on to something. I had always enjoyed beer, but now it seemed bigger to me somehow. I started to see how it brought people together. I started to feel how passionate people were about this simple liquid that could be shared and enjoyed by such a diverse sample of the population. I also realized I had the bug to brew.

As do many newbies in the chapters of history, I paid homage to my beer heroes…by knocking them off. I began home brewing my own Boston lager and hand-capping bottles that my roommate and I could take to parties. It wasn't bad. It wasn't great. The most important thing was that I was brewing my own beer. Soon I was swept up into the passionate world of craft beer, and there was no turning back.

What I came to realize later is that passion for great beer has been around for a long, long, long time. Beer has helped shape culture and society literally and figuratively, and one city in particular that had felt the impact of this golden elixir was Detroit. With more than forty production breweries, Detroit was the beer capital of the country from the late 1800s until Prohibition. Even during Prohibition, the spirit of Detroit beer lovers was hard to keep down. In fact, the idea of not having our beloved suds was not even an option for some—like the Purple Gang, whose members were notorious bootleggers who brought over barrels of liquid gold right down at the end of the block of where our brewery is located (Atwater and the Detroit River).

Memories of touring the Stroh's brewery and tasting freshly brewed beers in the taproom were part of the reason that I decided to relocate to Detroit in 1997. I knew that I wanted to be part of the renaissance of the city, and what better way to help bring back the city with such a long and storied past for brewing than infusing new life into it with a craft brewery.

I love lagers, so my vision is to create unique, delicious, refreshing German-style craft lagers. But another important part of my vision was to bring back the community side of beer—the idea of sitting down with friends at communal tables to enjoy great beer and great conversation. This is prevalent in Europe and especially Germany, but I believe it's an important thread in the social, cultural and economic impact of the craft. Getting to know your neighbor by sitting at a table and having a cold one. Solving the world's problems one pint at a time. Making friends and memories that will last a lifetime. It's a way of life that transcends generations, especially in Detroit, an intoxicating town that embraces creativity and diversity and welcomes anyone who brings that same energy.

It's far more than just a liquid. Beer has been, and still is, a magical elixir that lubricates many of the moving parts of society while at the same time bonding passionate people and communities together. Always has, always will. We're all just lucky enough to taste a small part of its history.

MARK RIETH
Owner of Atwater Brewery, Detroit

ACKNOWLEDGEMENTS

The phrase "It takes a village" is a great way to sum up the acknowledgements section of this book. Planning, researching, interviewing, writing, editing, arranging and taking pictures are big parts of a book project. Just as important, however, are the people who donated time and effort to help me with this project. First and foremost, I need to thank my wife, Laura Johnson, and my parents, George and Noreen Johnson. If it were not for their love, editing and support, I wouldn't have even considered tackling this project. I would also like to thank my friends for all of their support. Running a beer-related business and writing and researching a book at the same time means that I cannot always be there for everyday life events. I appreciate everyone's understanding. It's your family and friends who stand by you through thick and thin. I would like to thank all of the brewers, brewery owners and their staff members who gave me their time and provided valuable input and background information. Without them, this book wouldn't be possible. Last but not least, I would like to thank the beer enthusiasts in the great state of Michigan. I love being a part of such an enthusiastic, nice and helpful group of fans!

PREFACE

Detroit has come a long way from its modest beginnings in 1701 when Antoine Cadillac founded it. Detroit went from being a small fur trading post for the French to becoming an industrial powerhouse with the auto industry. Like other parts of the country, Detroit attracted immigrants from Europe and the rest of the world as they sought new opportunities. With them, they brought their own local food tastes and beer customs that were soon reflected on menus and beverage listings at local restaurants, bars and saloons.

From the mid-1800s to present day, Detroit has always had a rich and vibrant beer scene that reflected its cultural diversity. Today, Detroit continues to offer an amazing array of beer styles, from German to Belgian to American classics. We live in a truly great time for beer. Detroit has nationally award-winning breweries and brewpubs, as well as amazing beer festivals that draw thousands of people to the area each year. Detroit also has beer and food pairing events that educate attendees on tasty food and beverage choices to maximize their dining experience. Furthermore, the Detroit area has beer bars that make national top ten lists for their variety and service, as well as the quality of their product. Lastly, there are also beer tours that expose people to the Detroit area, take them to breweries for samplings and help others discover all the great places to imbibe.

This book tells the story of Detroit beer from the beginning of the small-scale brewers to the rise and fall of large-scale brewing and back to the rebirth of the local breweries of today. It will chronicle this all from the viewpoint of a Detroit native and beer lover. I hope you enjoy reading this book as much I did writing it.

Introduction

Beer has always been part of our culture in the United States and the rest of the world. From hunters and gatherers making beer from grain and water to civilized societies developing new styles, beer has been there as the life of the party. Beer has always been used as a celebratory drink. People drink it at birthdays, anniversaries, weddings, sporting events, funerals and other types of special celebrations and occasions.

As you may already know, beer is made up of water, malt, yeast and hops. Some ancient recipes for beer also include such ingredients as rice, maize, agave, sorghum, hay, mint, dandelion and even wormwood. Hops began to be used as a preservative for beer around AD 1000. In the 1200s, commercial breweries appeared in England, Germany and Austria. Beer was often used for trading, taxing and payment. In fact, wages were often paid in beer as part of the workingman's daily rations.

Germany passed the Reinheitsgebot beer purity law in 1516. It stated that it's illegal to use any ingredients other than water, barley and hops in the making of beer. Germany adjusted the law to include yeast as a fourth ingredient in the 1800s when Louis Pasteur discovered the role of yeast in fermentation. The law remained in effect in Germany until 1987. The Reinheitsgebot served as the oldest consumer protection law and was a guarantee of beer quality throughout Germany.

The history of beer in the United States began even before the English populated our great land. When Christopher Columbus came upon America's shores in the 1490s, he found Native Americans already making beer. In 1620, when the Pilgrims landed at Plymouth Rock, they chose that location in part because they were thirsty and had run out of beer. Beer was used as currency for trade between the early English settlers and the native Indians.

In this book, we will make references to a barrel of beer. A U.S. barrel of beer equals thirty-one gallons or 330 twelve-ounce beers. A "standard" keg is a half-barrel, or 15.5 gallons of beer.

THE BEGINNING OF BREWERIES IN DETROIT

1830s-1918

The dawn of breweries in Detroit started in the 1830s and 1840s. The early immigrants to Detroit were mostly English, Irish and Scottish. They brought over their customs, culture and cuisine, and that included beer. Ales were the styles that were already prevalent in their homelands. These are top-fermented beers that are typically malty beer styles that include amber, brown porter and stouts and require less aging than other beer types. Brewing technology was pretty crude in the 1800s. Storing and preserving ales during this period was challenging. Ale styles were effective in hiding any brewing imperfections that may have resulted from imperfect brewing techniques. Therefore, many brewers focused on these European styles.

Breweries in the 1830 and 1840s were typically smaller operations. Many brewers made beer in sheds, garages or in the rear of their homes or saloons. Early Detroit brewers, like the rest of country, would only brew enough beer to service their local saloon or saloons within the one- to two-block radius of where they lived. These brewers were more focused on brewing for a local community in small batches. The beer that was produced was sold on draft and typically served very cold. The first Detroit brewery on record was written about in an 1861 Detroit newspaper article, according to the book *Brewed in Detroit*. The newspaper article states that in 1837, the Davis & Moore Brewery was in operation at the corner of Atwater and Woodbridge Streets. By the late 1860s, nearly forty small brewers were active in downtown Detroit. This phase of brewing in Detroit during the nineteenth century was also mirrored by the period in the early 1990s in Detroit and the rebirth of craft beer. Both started with very small breweries serving a local population.

The next phase of breweries in Detroit came from the wave of German immigrants who arrived to the area from the 1860s to the 1880s. The Germans brought with them their love of lager beer styles. Lagers are bottom-fermented beers that take longer to age than ales and are brewed at colder temperatures. *Lager* means to store or age in German. Typical lager beer styles include helles, pilsner, bock, marzen, Vienna, dunkel and schwarz bier. By the end of the 1800s, the beer business had shifted away from the early smaller English, Irish and Scottish breweries. Consumers started to favor the clean lagers of the German breweries. The smaller breweries just couldn't keep up with the larger-scale operations as the German brewers began to erect larger brewhouses and made improvements in the overall brewing process. Commercial refrigeration truly ushered in the modern era of brewing in Detroit and the rest of the United States. Refrigeration replaced using ice for cooling and the practice of aging beer in icehouses. In 1857, Louis Pasteur established the key role of yeast as the microorganism responsible for alcoholic fermentation. Advancements in yeast cultures, a main ingredient of making beer, gave rise to breweries adding in-house laboratories to monitor and improve the consistency of their beer. In the late 1870s, Adolphus Busch pioneered the use of refrigerated railroad cars for long-distance shipping of beers. All of these advancements gave rise to 2,300 breweries in the United States in the 1800s. That peak number has just finally been passed during the current wave of craft brewery openings in the United States.

In the early 1900s, Detroit's beer industry was growing into a competitive local and regional participant in the nation's love of drinking beer. Prohibition was right around the corner and would put the entire beer industry in limbo. Detroit's beer industry, like the rest of the United States, was affected by the passing of Prohibition. It caused the closures of the majority of the nation's breweries, and many of these breweries were never to be reopened again.

Prohibition Years

1918-1933

Temperance Movement

In the early 1900s, the temperance movement in Michigan gathered a following, and by 1911, forty of Michigan's eighty-three counties had voted to go dry.

By 1916, the rest of Michigan went dry with the passing of the state amendment known as the Damon Act. It prohibited sales of liquor, beer and wine. The amendment was signed by Governor Albert Sleeper on May 1, 1917, and went into effect one year later on May 1, 1918. The Damon Act made Detroit the first city in the United States with a population over 250,000 to go dry. The one-year lag in implementing the Damon Act allowed people to stockpile huge quantities of beer, wine and liquor.

Nationally, Prohibition was enacted in 1919 via the Eighteenth Amendment, and enforcement began in 1920 with the passing of the Volstead Act. The act prohibited the manufacture, sale or transportation of intoxicating liquor. It permitted sales of non-intoxicating cider, fruit juices for home use and alcoholic beverages for medicinal, sacramental and industrial purposes. It was also still legal to produce wine for home use. In the first months of Prohibition, fifteen thousand physicians and fifty-seven thousand druggists applied for licenses to dispense liquor. The most common problem that people reported to their doctors was that they were having trouble sleeping. Hence, a bottle of booze was prescribed to solve the problem.

Above: "The Last Call" for liquor sales before the enforcement of the Eighteenth Amendment. *Courtesy of Walter P. Reuther Library.*

Left: Historic Prohibition-era photo. *Courtesy of Library of Congress.*

Historic Prohibition-era photo. *Courtesy of Library of Congress.*

The early passing of prohibition in Michigan was due to a variety of things. The "wets," which were made up of tavern owners, brewers and distillers, many of whom were German, were against prohibition. "Dry" groups included the Michigan Anti-Saloon League (founded in 1893) and several coalitions of church, community and business leaders who were also for prohibition. These dry groups mounted a very well-organized campaign in Michigan.

Many business leaders supported the view that widespread use of beer and liquor by workers sharply reduced productivity and increased absenteeism. Henry Ford took this view a step further by establishing a department to monitor the behavior of workers and their families to curb the use of alcohol. Excessive use of alcohol or drunkenness by an employee was a cause for dismissal at Ford Motor Company.

Michigan church leaders were long active in the temperance movement. During the months prior to the passing of statewide prohibition in 1916, Billy Sunday, a nationally known revivalist and evangelist, visited Detroit and made a famous "Booze Sermon." He was a former Major League Baseball player for the Chicago White Stockings, and he had already gained a national following for his stand on drinking. His speech, titled "Evils of Alcohol," was given in front of thousands of Michigan citizens in a large empty field at the corner of Cass Avenue and Woodward. "Liquor" he railed, "is the blood sucker of humanity; it is God's worst enemy and hell's best friend." The attacks were aimed at saloonkeepers, brewers and distillers.

TAKING OUT THE ALCOHOL

The origin of low-alcohol beer has its roots in European and United States history. "Small beer" is a beer that contains little alcohol and was produced for consumption by children and servants in medieval Europe. During this time in history, it was safer to drink beer than water. Water was known to carry many bacterial diseases and contaminants and lead to cholera, diarrhea and typhoid fever. The process of brewing beer pasteurizes the water, and the fermentation and hops protect against contamination. Drinking "small beer" instead of water was one way to guard against these and other waterborne diseases.

The temperance movement in the United States led to the development of beers that could be drunk without intoxicating effects. When the Eighteenth Amendment and the Volstead Act were passed in 1919 and 1920 in the United States, they permitted the sale of beers with .5 percent alcohol content. These beverages became known as "tonics" or "near beers," and many breweries began brewing these extremely low-alcohol content beverages in order to keep from going out of business during Prohibition. Due to the fact that removing the alcohol from the beer requires the addition of one simple step, many breweries saw this as an easy transition. In 1933, when

Prohibition was repealed, the majority of breweries ceased production of near beers and went back to making full-alcohol beers.

The most popular American near beers during Prohibition were Anheuser-Busch's Bevo, Pabst Brewing Company's Pablo, Miller Brewing's Vivo, Stroh Brewing Company's Lux-o and Schlitz Brewing's Famo. In most cases, these near beers did their job. They enabled the breweries that produced them to weather the storm of Prohibition and stay in business. Production of near beer had reached over 300 million gallons by 1921. However, the public never fully accepted the near beers due to the very funky taste. One popular illegal practice was to add alcohol to near beer. The resulting beverage was known as "spiked beer" or "needle beer." It was called this because a needle was used to inject alcohol through the cork of the bottle or keg. Today, the market for non-alcoholic beer in the United States is pretty small. According to Michigan law, a person must be eighteen or older to purchase non-alcoholic beer.

Prohibition-Related Terms

speakeasy: an establishment that illegally sold alcoholic beverages. The name "speakeasy" is coined from people's fear of being caught. Loud patrons were told to "speak easy."

blind pig: a working-class bar or saloon that sold alcoholic beverages illegally. The bar charged customers to see an exotic attraction and then served a complimentary alcoholic beverage and consequently sidestepped the law. It is also known as a "blind tiger."

gang: an organized group of criminals.

bootlegger: someone who illegally makes, distributes or sells liquor.

rumrunner: a person who illegally transported liquor in or out of an area. This was typically accomplished by boat, truck or car.

rackets: illegitimate businesses and other illegal operations. Examples include extortion, gambling, illegal bookmaking, hijacking, bootlegging and the numbers game.

teetotaler: a person who abstains from the consumption of alcohol. The phrase is believed to have originated within temperance societies. Members would add a *T* to their signatures to indicate total abstinence.

scofflaw: a person who illegally drank during the Prohibition era. The word loosely translates to someone who ridicules or deliberately violates the law (i.e., scoffs at the law).

flappers: women in the 1920s who showed their disdain for the traditional ways that women were expected to act in society. They enjoyed dressing fashionably, gambling, drinking, dancing and partying.

bathtub gin: a homemade gin that was mixed in a bathtub and was common during Prohibition. The phrase came to be used as a general term for any type of cheap homemade booze. White lightning was the whiskey equivalent of bathtub gin. Both were highly potent, illegally made and poor-quality spirits.

hooch: another slang term for liquor popularized during Prohibition. Unlike bathtub gin and white lightning, hooch has a history based in Alaska during colonial times. The origin of the term is said to come from the Hoochinoo Indians of Alaska. This tribe, in the nineteenth century, had a reputation for drunkenness and as a source for illicit liquor, which they distilled from molasses and other ingredients. The drink became associated with the tribe and was shortened to hooch.

Prohibition affected Detroit much harder than cities of its size elsewhere in the United States since Detroit and Michigan adopted prohibition two years earlier than the rest of the country. Consequently, after Prohibition, Michigan brewers were especially eager to start producing beer and return to the same lifestyle enjoyed prior to the temperance movement.

SPEAKEASIES OF DETROIT

The Rivertown-Warehouse District along the Detroit River was known for speakeasies and blind pigs during Prohibition in Detroit. The Woodbridge Tavern, the Tangerine Room, Soup Kitchen, Rivertown Saloon and the Rhino all operated during Prohibition, and they continued to operate from the 1960s to the 1980s, as this area was a popular bar and restaurant district.

Pre-prohibition Detroit had about 1,500 bars in the city. However, in 1925, it was estimated that 25,000 speakeasies and blind pigs existed in Detroit and that fifty thousand people were employed in the trade of illegal alcohol. During the Prohibition years, secret rooms in basements, homes, commercial buildings and garages were the new "bars" in Detroit.

Some bars still in business in Detroit today that once operated as speakeasies or blind pigs include the Stonehouse Bar at 19803 Ralston, Tommy's (Little Harry's) at 624 Third Street, Two Way Inn at 17897 Mount Elliott Street, Nancy Whiskey's Pub at 2644 Harrison Street, Cadieux Café at 4300 Cadieux Road and Ye Olde Tap Room at 14915 Charlevoix Street.

Prohibition-era speakeasy. *Courtesy of Walter P. Reuther Library.*

DETROIT BEER

Prohibition-Era Gangs in Detroit

During the Prohibition era (1918–33), various gangs and mobs representing many European ethnic groups scrambled to grab a piece of the profit to be made selling illegal liquor in the Detroit area. Their activities expanded to other "rackets" as well, and eventually turf issues developed among the various mobs and gangs. Soon, mob/gang wars, crime and violence were common occurrences on the streets of Detroit.

The Purple Gang

The most famous Detroit gang during Prohibition was the Purple Gang. It called the Rivertown-Warehouse District/Eastern Market area its home turf. The "Purples" were a loose confederation of mostly Jewish gangsters and were led by the four Bernstein brothers: Abe, Joe, Ray and Izzy. They were involved in all kinds of rackets, including hijacking, extortion, protection and gambling.

By 1929, the Purple Gang controlled the Detroit-area underworld to the point that pretty much no underworld operation went on in the Detroit area without kicking back protection money to the Purple Gang. Its members were also selling liquor to the New York Mob and Al Capone in Chicago. By 1930, at least five hundred murders had been attributed to the Purples.

The Purple Gang members were known for being hijackers, particularly of Canadian whisky. Hijacking involved stealing a load of liquor and killing everybody who had been carrying the load. The Purple Gang would then take the good-quality Canadian whisky and "cut it" or dilute it. A good bottle of whisky could be made into three bottles of cut product.

During the late 1920s, the Purple Gang was involved in protection of the cleaning and dyeing industry. If cleaners and tailors resisted such protection, the Purple Gang would break windows, throw dye on clothing and burn the buildings. One rumor had it that it got its colorful name because members sometimes threw purple dye on clothing. Another legend maintains that the Purple Gang received its name as a result of a conversation between two shopkeepers. Jewish kids in Eastern Market had terrorized both shops. One of the shopkeepers exclaimed, "These boys are not like other children of their age; they're tainted, off color. They're rotten, purple like the color of bad meat. They're a purple gang."

By 1935, eighteen of the Purple Gang members had been killed by other members of their own gang. Of the four Bernstein brothers who were gang leaders, Ray spent thirty years in prison and died in 1966; Abe eventually ended up in Miami, where he died in 1968; and Joe and Izzy moved to California and became legitimate businessmen.

Giannola/Vitale Gang

The Giannola Gang was in control of the Italian/Sicilian underworld in Detroit, Ecorse and Wyandotte. When Prohibition came along in 1918 in Michigan, the Giannola Gang became involved in rumrunning and hijacking trucks and cars, bringing contraband liquor into Michigan. One of its favorite targets was U.S. 25, known as "Dixie Highway," a popular route for transporting liquor from Toledo to Detroit. The sixty-mile-long road became known as "Rum Runners Runway" and "Avenue De Booze." The gang also used boats to transport liquor from Canada across the Detroit River to Ecorse and Wyandotte.

In early 1918, Giovanni "John" Vitale, a Giannola lieutenant, broke away from the Giannola Gang and formed his own Vitale Gang. When the two gangs began stealing from each other, an all-out war erupted. In early 1919, Tony Giannola was killed by a Vitale spy. In late 1919, Sam Giannola was killed as he walked out of a bank on the corner of Russell and Monroe Streets.

In August 1920, John Vitale's son was killed in a botched assassination attempt on John. One month later, John Vitale was en route to Michigan Central Station to supposedly make a liquor deal when he was killed by several gunmen with sawed-off shotguns at 241 Fourteenth Street.

The "Giannola/Vitale Gang War" finally ended in late 1920 since most of the leaders of both gangs had been killed. There would be a ten-year truce between Sicilian and Italian mobs until 1930, when the "Crosstown Mob War" between the eastside and westside mobs erupted.

The River Gang

After the bloody Giannola/Vitale Gang War among the Italians in 1920, the remnants of both groups formed into several independent gangs. Each gang was given the right to operate within its own geographic area in Metro

Detroit. Disputes between the various groups were arbitrated and resolved by a small council composed mostly of widely respected leaders of the local Sicilian underworld, including Sam Catalanotte.

The River Gang was one of the Italian gangs that formed as a result of the gang war. The River Gang ran the rumrunning activities of the upper Detroit River between the eastern limits of Detroit and Mount Clemens during Prohibition. It stayed outside Detroit due to the tight control of the Purple Gang. The River Gang made its money by carrying loads of other rumrunners in its boats across the Detroit River.

In the late 1920s, the majority of the independent rumrunners were paying protection money to the River Gang. Part of the River Gang's success was its ability to bribe the United States custom officials. Unfortunately, one evening at a local Detroit bar, a U.S. customs official drank too much and bragged about being on the River Gang's payroll. Detroit police stopped the River Gang's leader in December 1929 on the Belle Isle Bridge. A shootout occurred, and Pete Licavoli, the River Gang's leader, narrowly escaped. He eventually turned himself in a month later and was sentenced to two years in Leavenworth Prison.

Italian Mafia/Detroit Mafia

A new Italian mafia family emerged to take control of the Detroit underworld just prior to Prohibition being repealed. In addition to "Italian Mafia," it was known by various names, including "Detroit Mafia" and "Detroit La Cosa Nostra." Four of the five original members of its first ruling commission were former leaders of the River Gang and the Eastside Mob.

When Prohibition was repealed in 1933, the liquor rackets were quickly replaced by the Depression-era demand for gambling rackets, and the newly formed Detroit Mafia family was there to cash in. By the early 1960s, the Detroit Mafia was making an estimated $150 million per year from gambling, narcotics, loan sharking, labor racketeering and extortion.

For more than fifty years, the Detroit Mafia was able to control the Detroit underworld and maintain a low profile while reaping fantastic profits in both legitimate businesses and the rackets. Finally, in the 1990s, a federal assault on the Detroit Mafia using the RICO (Racketeer Influenced & Corrupt Organizations) law marked the beginning of the end for the old-style Detroit Mafia.

A HISTORY OF BREWING IN THE MOTOR CITY

The "Detroit Partnership" is what the local Detroit mafia calls itself today, and it has about forty to fifty known members. Although it is smaller in size than in the time of Prohibition, it is still considered one of the top criminal organizations within Michigan.

Detroit Mobs/Gangs
(Primarily During the Prohibition Era from 1918 to 1933)

Name of Mob/ Gang	Predominant Ethnic Group	Primary Years of Operation	Main Areas of Operation	Primary Rackets
Giannola Gang and Vitale Gang	Italian	1911–20	Detroit area	Various
Eastside Mob and Westside Mob	Italian	1921–30	East-Upper Detroit River	Rumrunning
Purple Gang	Jewish	1920–35	Detroit area	All Rackets
Jaworski Gang/ Flathead Mob	Polish	1923–29	Hamtramck	Robberies
River Gang	Italian	1925–30	north and south of Detroit city limits	Rumrunning
Kozak Gang	Polish	1925–26	southeastern Michigan	Robberies
Legs Laman Gang	Irish	1926–30	Detroit area	Kidnapping
Detroit La Cosa Nostra	Italian	1930–90	Detroit Metro area	All Rackets

SMUGGLING AND CANADA

The Detroit River is a narrow thirty-two-mile stretch of water that was full of hiding spots for the smuggling of illegal alcohol. The Detroit River spans from the southern harbor facilities of Grosse Ile, Wyandotte, Ecorse and

River Rouge all the way north to Lake St. Clair. Smugglers used boats, but cars and even ice skates were used to cross the Detroit River when it was frozen. Enforcement of Prohibition was shared between federal, state and local government agencies. These included the U.S. Customs, U.S. Coast Guard, the Prohibition Unit of the Bureau of Internal Review and the local and state police.

Canada was expected to embrace prohibition in 1920. However, instead of passing it, Canada levied a nine-dollar-per-gallon tax on whisky. Despite the huge increase, the tax did little to stem the tide of rumrunning across the Detroit River. Canada eventually passed countrywide prohibition in 1929.

In 1920, the Detroit police had limited resources for enforcement and only one boat for patrols on the Detroit River. Thus, the Detroit River became a smugglers' paradise. Seized boats were sold at auction, often being purchased by the same people from whom they were confiscated in the first place. During the 1920s, thousands of boats were licensed in Michigan. Detroit was considered a leading manufacturer of marine engines, and 90 percent of all liquor illegally imported into Michigan was by boat. The boats differed widely in size, type, shape and appearance. Steamers, tugs, motorboats, sailboats, rowboats and even canoes were employed. All of these boats were used to employ evasive tactics and at times high speeds to dodge the police boats waiting on the far shore.

Several million cases of Canadian liquor came into Detroit each year. It has been written that 75 percent of the illegal booze that came into the United States came via the Detroit River. Only 5 percent of the liquor was ever seized. Most confiscated liquor was dumped into the Detroit River or Lake St. Clair. By 1929, illegal liquor was the second-biggest business in Detroit at $216 million per year. The illegal booze trade was second only to the auto industry in profits.

Smuggling has always been a way of life in border cities. During Prohibition, sneaking liquor across the border between Canada and Michigan was almost a badge of honor. It was estimated that up to 25 percent of the local population in Windsor, Canada, was involved in some form of smuggling alcohol into Detroit.

Hiram Walker founded his distillery in 1858 in Detroit. He first learned how to distill cider vinegar in his grocery store in the 1830s before moving on to whiskey and producing his first barrels in 1854. However, with the prohibition movement gathering momentum and Michigan already becoming "dry," Walker decided to move his distillery across the Detroit River to Windsor, Ontario. From there, he was able to export his whiskey, continue to perfect the distillation process and start to develop the town of Walkerville, which later became part of Windsor. The Hiram Walker distillery remains in production today and is now owned by the Beam Suntory Company. Beam Suntory also owns Jim Beam. You can visit the Canadian Club welcome center for tours, learn about the nearby distillery and enjoy a sample.

Detroit police arrested 34,000 people for liquor violations from 1918 to 1928, but only 25 percent were actually convicted. In 1924, the United States and Canada signed a treaty to control liquor coming into the United States. Canada would notify the United States when clearance was granted to a U.S. vessel picking up liquor at Canadian export docks. However, this did little to curb the smuggling. Rumrunners just changed names on boats and followed odd routes to avoid the Coast Guard. From 1927 to 1938, 750 Coast Guard employees were dismissed for misconduct, and 550 were charged with extortion and bribery.

In 1929, Ottawa closed down all export docks on the Detroit River. Thus, smugglers moved over to Lake St. Clair and Lake Huron with their boats and used different routes to avoid the Coast Guard. Smugglers also began using planes and trains to get their product over the river.

By the early 1930s, the public had grown tired of the violence, bribery and collusion of the police force. Prohibition had failed to curb drinking in the United States, and the public wanted the crime and violence to end. The United States was in an economic depression, with 46 percent unemployed in 1931. The political machine kicked into high gear, and the Democrats campaigned that repealing Prohibition would bring new jobs created in the taverns, breweries and distillery industries. The Democrats won the 1932 elections, and Prohibition ceased shortly after.

President Franklin D. Roosevelt signed the Cullen-Harrison Act on March 22, 1933. It authorized the sale of 3.2 percent beer, a beer thought to have too low an alcohol concentration to be intoxicating.

On May 10, 1933, at the American Legion Convention in Detroit, one thousand glasses were rented to celebrate the first 3.2 percent beer served in Detroit. During the party that evening, three hundred barrels and five hundred cases of Stroh beer were consumed.

On April 10, 1933, Michigan was the first state to ratify the Twenty-first Amendment, the repeal of Prohibition. The Twenty-first Amendment was fully ratified and thus became a law on December 5, 1936, after the thirty-sixth state (Utah) ratified the amendment, which achieved the requisite three-fourths majority of states' approval. Some states continued

Historic Detroit downtown streets. *Courtesy of the Library of Congress.*

Historic Detroit downtown.
Courtesy of the Library of Congress.

local prohibition within their jurisdictions. Almost two-thirds of all states adopted some form of local option, which enabled residents to vote for or against local prohibition. For a time, 38 percent of Americans lived in areas with prohibition. By 1966, however, all states had repealed their statewide prohibition laws.

The Golden Age of Large-Scale Breweries

1933-1990s

May 11, 1933, officially kicked off the next era of brewing in Detroit and the nation. Prohibition caused all brewers to stop producing and selling alcoholic beverages in Detroit from 1918 to 1933. Legally making and selling 3.2 percent beer was the first part of the repeal of Prohibition. The Cullen-Harrison Act was enacted on May 11, 1933, and authorized the sale of 3.2 percent beer. The remaining parts of the Eighteenth Amendment would not be officially repealed until December 5, 1933. Legal beer was good news for the brewing industry in Detroit. In the year following repeal, sixteen breweries started up or reopened in the city of Detroit, but by 1938, Detroit had only ten breweries remaining. In the 1940s and 1950s, breweries started purchasing one another, and eventually only one company remained in Detroit: Stroh Brewery Company. This chapter profiles these ten breweries and the period of large-scale brewing in the city of Detroit.

STROH BREWERY COMPANY

The first generation of Stroh family brewers started with Johann Peter Stroh in 1775 in Kirn, Germany. Johann and his family lived in a house with an adjoining brewhouse attached, and they ran a local inn that served meals and beer. Johann had three sons and one daughter. His second son, Georg Friedrich, inherited the brewhouse. Georg's youngest son was Johann

Historic brewhouse. *Courtesy of Atwater Brewery.*

Bernhard Stroh, who was born in 1821, and he also learned the brewing trade. Unfortunately, the brewhouse could only support one family, and with unrest occurring in Germany, Bernhard Stroh immigrated to the United States in 1848.

It has always been stated within Stroh Brewery's archives that Bernhard Stroh founded the brewery of B. Stroh in Detroit in 1850. Since there were no federal licenses and state regulations at that time, the exact founding date remains somewhat of a mystery. In 1875, Lion Brewing Company became the brewery's name. Bernhard Stroh adopted the Lion's Crest as the logo for his new brewery. It was based on the crest from his hometown in Kirn, Germany. Bernhard Stroh's son, Bernhard Stroh Jr., took charge of the brewery upon the death of his father in 1882, and he changed the brewery's name to the B. Stroh Brewing Company. The name was subsequently changed to Stroh Brewery Company in 1902. In 1908, Bernhard Stroh Jr.'s brother, Julius, took over the brewery. In 1911, Stroh began brewing from copper kettles heated by gas. The fire-brewing process uses a direct flame rather than steam to heat beer-filled copper kettles. The resulting higher temperatures intensified the aroma and the body of the beer, resulting in a more flavorful brew. This process, common in parts of Europe, became known as "Stroh's fire-brewed beer." Stroh Brewery Company was the only brewery in America at that time brewing beer in this way. The company marketed this beer under the brand Stroh's Bohemian Style Beer, and the beer can read "America's only fire brewed beer."

Above: The B. Stroh Brewing Company, 1885. *From* Stroh's: The Fire Brewing Story.

Left: Bernhard Stroh photo. *From* Stroh's: The Fire Brewing Story.

Bernhard Stroh grave site. *Photo by Stephen Johnson.*

Since beer was outlawed during Prohibition, Stroh Brewery Company changed its name to the Stroh Products Company and produced sodas, near beer (non-alcoholic beer), malted hop syrup and ice cream.

The closing of saloons across the nation opened up a new opportunity for Stroh Products Company. Ice cream saloons (parlors) increased in popularity as a new place for the average person to frequent. Stroh decided to convert the beer brewing facilities of its brewhouse in Detroit to producing ice cream under the Alaska brand name. At the end of Prohibition in 1933, the ice cream operation proved to be so popular and profitable that Stroh continued to produce ice cream and changed the brand name to Stroh's Ice Cream.

In the early 1980s, Stroh's built an ice cream production facility where the former Goebel Brewing plant had once stood. Stroh sold the ice cream facility in 1989 to Melody Farms as a part of corporate restructuring. Melody Farms ran Stroh's Ice Cream for several years until Dean Foods purchased that company in 2005. Dean Foods continued to use the plant to produce ice cream until 2007, when it moved production of Stroh's Ice Cream to a newer plant in Belvidere, Illinois. Stroh's Ice Cream no longer has any direct ties to the city of Detroit.

Stroh's Ice Cream site. *Photo by Stephen Johnson.*

While the ice cream business kept Stroh afloat during Prohibition, the repeal of Prohibition in 1933 was a welcome sign for the company. Julius Stroh was now president and returned the company's name from Stroh Products Company back to Stroh Brewery Company. On May 10, 1933, Julius Stroh tapped the first legal barrel of beer at a special celebration with the American Legion in Detroit. That epic party kicked off the next phase of growth at Stroh Brewery Company, and by 1936, Stroh was producing 700,000 barrels of beer annually. Upon Julius Stroh's death in 1939, his son Gari took over as the president of Stroh Brewery Company. Gari's brother, John Stroh, became president in 1950.

During the 1950s, the Stroh business was in serious decline. Two factors contributed to this situation. First, changing consumer tastes were shifting from the full-flavored beers produced by Stroh toward light beers. Secondly, increasing competition from the Detroit breweries of Goebel Brewing Company and Pfeiffer Brewing Company started stealing market share away from Stroh. Both of these factors, as well as strong advertising by its competition, caused Stroh to make changes to the way it ran the company.

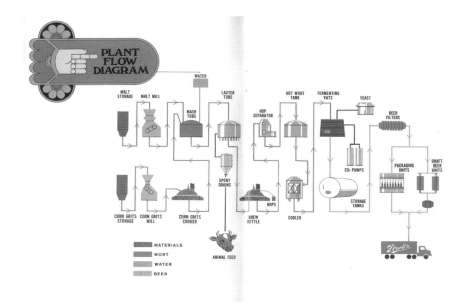

Above: Stroh's Brewery plant flow diagram. *From* Stroh's: The Fire Brewing Story.

Right: Stroh's beer coasters and bottle cap. *Photo by Noreen Johnson.*

In 1964, Stroh acquired Goebel Brewing and thereby eliminated one of its chief competitors. Stroh also made changes in the form of management. In 1967, Peter Stroh became president of Stroh Brewery Company, and he worked to put Stroh in a position to flourish.

Prior to Prohibition, saloons were the dominant legal retail outlets for alcohol, and manufacturers owned bars to distribute their product on-tap. After Prohibition, manufacturers had to sell to wholesalers and could not own bars. This did not work to the advantage of the small brewer. Larger breweries increased sales because of two important trends in homes in the United States. The factors were the spread of home refrigeration (more easily keeping the product cold) and television viewing (where viewers were exposed to the expensive national advertising campaigns done by large beer companies). The larger cost meant that the amount of beer a brewery had to produce in order to survive doubled in just ten years. Due to these trends and the emergence of Anheuser-Busch and Miller Brewing as leaders in the beer industry, Stroh Brewery Company had to become a much larger brewery in order to stay profitable.

In 1972, Stroh was the eighth-largest brewery in the United States, selling 4 million barrels of beer per year and extending its reach into seventeen states. Under the direction of Peter Stroh, the company moved into a period of major changes to its business model. Stroh acquired Schaefer Brewing out of New York in 1981 and Schlitz Brewing out of Wisconsin in 1982. The combined breweries meant that Stroh ranked third in national beer sales with more than 24 million barrels of beer produced at its peak. Stroh Brewery Company spent heavily in an attempt to transform the Stroh brand into a premium national brand against the deeper pockets of Anheuser-Busch and Miller.

The Stroh brewery in Detroit was finally closed in 1985. With the recent acquisitions, the Detroit plant had become outdated. In 1987, Stroh redeveloped its former Detroit brewery and headquarters into a modern office complex known as Brewery Park. Today, Crain Communications occupies the building. Stroh moved its headquarters over to Stroh River Place, which was formerly the home of the Detroit-based pharmaceutical firm Parke Davis & Company. The buildings date back to the early twentieth century. The Stroh family purchased the historically designated site in 1979. Peter Stroh oversaw the restoration of fifteen historic buildings. Stroh River Place is composed of more than 500,000 square feet and includes a parking structure, three hundred residences, office space, Roberts Riverwalk Hotel (formerly the Omni) and the Rattlesnake Club restaurant. The retail building

Former Stroh Brewery site. Today, it is home to Crain's Communications. *Photo by Stephen Johnson.*

served as the corporate headquarters and laboratory for Stroh Brewery Company after 1985.

In the early 1990s, Stroh contract-brewed for microbreweries including Boston Beer Company and Pete's Wicked Ale. Contract brewing proved to be a lucrative business for Stroh, since microbreweries needed larger breweries' facilities to help them increase brewing capacity and thereby enter new markets. In the 1990s, contract brewing at Stroh accounted for nearly 25 percent of its business. A contract brewery is a brewery that brews beer in its brewhouse by contract. Frequently, smaller breweries use contract breweries to get additional product out in the market. Smaller breweries do not always have the capacity or capital or both to expand. Thus, contract brewers fill that void in the market.

In 1996, Stroh acquired G. Heileman Brewing Company out of Wisconsin. This brewery purchase of more than thirty brands meant that Old Style, Colt 45, National Bohemian, Black Label, Blatz, Olympia, Rainier brands and more were added to the Stroh product line. As a result of the G. Heileman purchase, Stroh Brewery Company was loaded with too much debt. Just one year shy of its 150th anniversary, the end of Stroh Brewery Company finally came on February 8, 1999. John Stroh III, who was then president, agreed to sell off the Stroh Brewery Company to the Pabst Brewing Company and Miller Brewing Company. Miller Brewing bought the Henry Weinhard's and Mickey's Malt Liquor brands. Pabst Brewing Company purchased the remaining brands including Stroh's Beer and Stroh's Light Beer. Both beers are still offered today in select markets, including Detroit. The others brands acquired by Pabst Brewing Company included Old Milwaukee, Schlitz, Schaefer, Old Style, Schmidt's, Lone Star, Special Export, McSorley's, Schlitz Malt Liquor and Rainier.

In 2014, Pabst Brewery Company was sold to Blue Ribbon Intermediate Holdings LLC, a partnership between Eugene Kashper and San Francisco–based investment fund TSG Consumer Partners LLC. Eugene Kashper runs the Russian-based Oasis Beverages that operates breweries in Russia, Ukraine, Belarus and Kazakhstan. Pabst Brewing Company is based in Los Angeles. Like Anheuser-Busch, Miller and Coors, Stroh is now in the hands of a foreign owner.

Today, not even a historical marker designates the site of the former Stroh Brewery Company headquarters. The marker was stolen and eventually recovered from someone in Florida trying to sell it on eBay. That marker is in storage in Lansing, Michigan. It reads:

> *Leaving the chaos of the 1848 German Revolution, Bernhard Stroh emigrated from Kirn, Germany, to South America. He soon decided to try his fortune in another German settlement, and in 1850 he arrived in Detroit. Trained as a brewer, Stroh opened a brewery on Catherine Street that same year.*
>
> *He developed a market for a new light lager beer among the larger German immigrant population. Pushing a cart through the city, he sold his beer from door to door. At his death in 1882 the Lion Brewery had become a thriving business to pass on to his sons, Julius and Bernhard Jr. They expanded the company and in 1902 changed the name to the Stroh Brewery Company. Today members of the Stroh family still manage what is one of Michigan's major family businesses.*

Unfortunately, the 1999 sale of Stroh Brewery Company marked the end of the Stroh family's involvement in the beer business and the end of an important part of Detroit's beer history.

A HISTORY OF BREWING IN THE MOTOR CITY

PFEIFFER BREWING COMPANY

Conrad Pfeiffer emigrated from Germany to America in 1871 at the age of seventeen. It wasn't until he was twenty-seven that he formally got started in the brewing industry by working for the Phillip Kling Brewery in Detroit. In 1892, Conrad started brewing beer with his nephew, Martin Breitmeyer, under the name Conrad Pfeiffer and Company. The Breitmeyers were a wealthy family as a result of their florist business and provided the necessary financial backing to start a brewery. In 1902, the company was reincorporated as the C. Pfeiffer Brewing Company.

C. Pfeiffer Brewing Company erected a large brewhouse on Detroit's eastside. Pfeiffer produced a Wurzburger beer, an export beer and a traditional lager called Pfeiffer's Famous Beer. The brewery was located between Beaufait and Bellevue and bordered by Mack Avenue on the outskirts of downtown Detroit. Train tracks running along the middle of the block allowed for easy deliveries and shipments and proved to be an initial advantage for Pfeiffer. Most other Detroit breweries relied on conventional but less efficient truck deliveries. A horse stable, an office building and a hospitality area were also built on the site.

Conrad Pfeiffer died in 1911 at the age of fifty-seven. After Conrad's death, his wife, Luisa Pfeiffer, and her daughter, Lillian, took control of the company.

Due to Michigan's early entry into prohibition, production at the brewery stopped in 1918, and the building sat idle. After Prohibition, a new firm was incorporated using the Pfeiffer Brewing Company name but with no members of the founding family. Production at the brewery resumed in 1934, and in that year, Pfeiffer ranked third in beer production in Detroit behind Stroh and Schmidt. In 1935, beer volume production nearly doubled to 200,000 barrels.

Alfred Epstein was chosen to run Pfeiffer Brewing Company. He set out to transform the brewery into a well-oiled brewing machine. After extensive post-Prohibition construction and expansion, the Pfeiffer Brewing Company occupied nearly the entire block. In the 1940s, a bottling facility and an office building were built, and beer sales during this period increased to 400,000 barrels.

Due to the rationing in World War II, breweries were forced by the government to stop canning beer to save steel for the war effort. Thus, bottled beer was all that was available to the general public until the end of the war. Pfeiffer Brewing Company was commissioned to produce canned beer for the government since beer cans were lighter, more durable and easier to ship overseas than bottles. In 1943, all breweries were required to contribute 15 percent of production for military use.

After the war, Pfeiffer Brewing Company made its cans available to the public, and for the first time, the Pfeiffer mascot, Johnny Fifer, appeared on cans. The company created an extensive advertising campaign centered on its mascot, which had been created and designed by the Walt Disney Studios.

From 1947 to 1958, 185 breweries closed or sold out to larger companies. According to the book *Brewed in Detroit*, this period has been called the "Great Shakeout." Pfeiffer Brewing Company experienced amazing growth, and sales reached 2 million barrels. To increase production, Pfeiffer Brewing Company purchased the now vacant Kling Brewery of Flint in 1947 and used that brewery to produce draft beer.

During the 1950s, Pfeiffer Brewing Company was the best-selling brand in Michigan. Pfeiffer produced a low-price beer, which made the Pfeiffer brew a popular choice among cost-conscious beer drinkers. In 1954, Pfeiffer Brewing Company acquired the Minnesota-based Jacob Schmidt Brewing Company.

The brewery workers strike in Detroit in 1958 affected all of the breweries in Detroit. This strike provided the opportunity for breweries from other states to enter the local market. Because of acquired debt from recent purchases, the Pfeiffer Brewing Company closed its Flint branch in 1958.

With increasing competition from out-of-market breweries, Pfeiffer Brewing Company made the choice to become a regional brewery. In 1962, it purchased the E&B Brewing Company. Pfeiffer Brewing Company renamed itself Associated Brewing Company, and it continued buying breweries in other markets, including Drewery's in South Bend, Indiana, and Chicago and Sterling in Evansville, Indiana, and Piel, with plants in New York and Massachusetts. The Associated Brewery was headquartered in Detroit. Pfeiffer Beer was still brewed at the Detroit brewery along with such old favorites as Frankenmuth, Schmidt and North Star. During this time, Pfeiffer beer was also brewed in St. Paul, Minnesota. Associated Brewing Company was now the tenth-largest brewery in the United States with nearly 4 million barrels.

The mounting debt from acquiring other breweries led Associated Brewing Company to close down the Pfeiffer Brewery property in Detroit in 1966. Due to lower excise taxes, it became cheaper to brew beer in Indiana. Associated Brewing Company continued producing Pfeiffer Beer until 1972.

In 1972, G. Heileman Brewing Company purchased the Pfeiffer Brewing name. Stroh Brewery Company purchased G. Heileman Brewing Company in 1996. However, Stroh never brewed Pfeiffer beer, and the brand vanished from the marketplace. The former Pfeiffer Brewing Company was renamed

Pfeiffer Brewing Company site. *Photo by Stephen Johnson.*

the Armada Corporation. The block of buildings that made up Pfeiffer Brewing Company was divided into several sections. A bus repair shop and a shipping company use some sections of the former Pfeiffer Brewing Company. All that remains today of the Pfeiffer Brewing Company are the original stables with a small adjoining office area.

GOEBEL BREWING COMPANY

In 1856, August Goebel left Germany at the age of seventeen. He was headed for Chicago when he ran out of funds and landed in Detroit, where he began working at a bookbindery. August Goebel also served in the Civil War, during which he rose through the ranks and eventually became Colonel Goebel. In 1870, August Goebel served as the superintendent of public works in Detroit, and finally, in 1873, Goebel and his partner, Theodore

August Goebel grave site. *Photo by Stephen Johnson.*

Gorenflo, founded A. Goebel & Company brewery. Within five years, they were selling nine thousand barrels annually.

An investment in 1890 by a British syndicate helped form a larger brewing operation for Goebel, and the Goebel Brewing Company was incorporated with August Goebel as the president. A new brewery was built at Rivard and Maple Streets in Detroit. The new brewery was a five-story brewhouse that rivaled Stroh Brewery Company, which was literally across the street.

August and his wife, Sophie, had eleven children, four of whom died young. In 1912, their sons August Jr. and Fritz joined Goebel Brewing Company. Prohibition in 1918 forced Goebel Brewing Company to close. The British syndicate had sold out to some local investors and renamed the company Detroit Industries Building. The brewery was rented out to manufacturing tenants during Prohibition. The only Goebel left in the business was Ted Goebel, the grandson of founder August Goebel. Production at the newly formed Goebel Brewing Company finally resumed in 1934, and sales at Goebel were brisk, reaching 367,000 barrels in 1935.

During the 1930s, Goebel started using the advertising slogan "From the Cypress Casks of Goebel." The slogan was in reference to the two large

Goebel Brewing horse-drawn beer delivery. *Courtesy of Walter P. Reuther Library.*

420-barrel copper brew kettles that Goebel used to brew its beer. Due to the anti-German sentiment that existed in the United States after World War II, Goebel changed its logo from a German eagle to an American bald eagle. At that same time, Goebel launched a new mascot called "Brewster Rooster." Using the Brewster Rooster, the bantam (so named because of the smaller-sized bottle) found a niche in the market as the odd-sized seven-ounce bottle. Goebel marketed the following beer brands: Goebel, Gold Label, Pils and Bantam Beers.

In 1948, Goebel Brewing Company purchased Koppitz-Melcher Brewing and used the newly acquired plant to expand production. In 1953, Goebel sales production peaked at 1.3 million barrels of beer. However, Stroh Brewery Company started to surpass Goebel in sales during the 1950s, and by 1960, Goebel's beer sales were in a tailspin. The cost to produce beer at Goebel's plant in Detroit had become too high. Competitors from outside the market could deliver beer in Detroit at a lower cost than Goebel. In 1964, Stroh acquired Goebel Brewing Company and all of its plants. Most of these plants were closed, used for other purposes or demolished. Stroh continued to sell Goebel beer as a lower-priced option in the marketplace. With little to no advertising, Goebel was able to recover to nearly 250,000 barrels sold

Goebel beer label. *Photo by Noreen Johnson.*

annually. It was sold by the case in bottles and cans. In the mid- to late '70s, a case of twenty-four bottles cost $4.44, not including the dollar refund when all empties were returned. When Pabst Brewing Company acquired Stroh's in 1999, it also got Goebel beer in the process. Pabst Brewing Company continued to sell Goebel until it eventually was discontinued in 2005, and that was the end of the Goebel beer story.

KOPPITZ-MELCHER BREWING COMPANY

Austrian-born Konrad Koppitz immigrated to Chicago at age nineteen. Konrad attended the Wahl-Henius Brewing Institute in Chicago and did some additional brewing studies in Germany. In 1884, Konrad and his wife, Emilie, along with their son, Benjamin, moved to Detroit, and Konrad became the new brewmaster for Stroh. At Stroh, Konrad met Arthur Melcher, who was a relative to Julius Stroh by marriage.

Both Konrad and Arthur left Stroh in 1890 to form the Koppitz-Melcher Brewing Company. They built the original sixty-thousand-barrel brewery

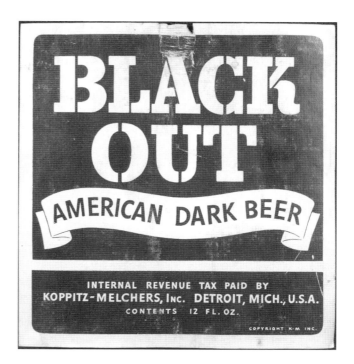

Black Out American Dark beer label. *Photo by Noreen Johnson.*

Black Velvet beer label. *Photo by Noreen Johnson.*

on Gratiot Avenue down the road from Goebel and Stroh. The building resembled a castle and was in operation from 1890 to 1918. It closed during Prohibition, and Faygo now owns the property.

Konrad Koppitz's son re-formed the company after Prohibition ended and built a 200,000-barrel plant at the foot of the Detroit River on Dubois Street. The company's brands included Koppitz Pale Select and Koppitz Silver Star. It sold the plant in 1947 to Goebel, which used it as a production facility. The Detroit River plant and the twenty-nine remaining Koppitz plants were demolished when Stroh purchased Goebel in 1964.

SCHMIDT BREWING COMPANY

Frank Schmidt and Joseph Kaiser founded Schmidt Brewing Company, originally known as Champion Brewery, in 1895. They renamed it Schmidt Products Company during Prohibition and leased the plant to Acme Beverage Company, which made hop-flavored malt syrup. After Prohibition, the Schmidt Products Company was re-formed as Schmidt Brewing Company with Frank Schmidt's sons, George and Frank Jr., heading the new company. They made Schmidt's Famous beer. Schmidt Brewing Company's claim to fame was that it had "no sugar" and "no glucose." It was marketed as "The Natural Beer," which was meant to stress that it was nonfattening. At its peak, Schmidt Brewing Company produced 300,000 barrels of beer annually. Schmidt Brewing Company closed in 1951, and E&B brewery purchased Schmidt Brewing Company in 1952. Schmidt Brewing Company once had buildings on the outer edge of Eastern Market that stretched the whole block from St. Aubin to where the Dequindre Cut rail-trail crosses Wilkins Street today, but little exists from the original structure.

Many breweries had names similar to Schmidt Brewing Company of Detroit. Schmidt Beer of St. Paul, Minnesota, was formed in 1900, and Schmidt's Brewing of Philadelphia, Pennsylvania, was formed in 1860. Pfeiffer Brewing Company in Detroit purchased Schmidt Beer of St. Paul in 1954. Pfeiffer Brewing Company purchased E&B Brewery of Detroit in 1963 and formed a new entity called Associated Brewing. G. Heileman Brewing Company purchased Associated Brewing in 1972. Schmidt's Brewing of Philadelphia was sold to G. Heileman Brewing Company in 1987. Stroh Brewing Company purchased G. Heileman Brewing Company in 1996. Stroh Brewing Company was sold to Pabst Brewing Company and

Schmidt's beer label. *Photo by Noreen Johnson.*

Miller Brewing Company in 1999. Confused? A lot of musical chairs games were being played.

Pabst Brewing Company essentially owns the rights to Schmidt Brewing Company of Detroit, Schmidt Beer of St. Paul and Schmidt's Brewing of Philadelphia. Pabst Brewing Company currently only sells Schmidt Beer in the Minnesota market today.

Detroit Brewing Company

In 1874, three Martz brothers—Frank, Michael and John—opened the Martz Brothers Brewery. The brothers incorporated under the final name

Detroit Brewing Company site. *Photo by Stephen Johnson.*

Oldbru beer label. *Photo by Noreen Johnson.*

of Detroit Brewing Company in 1886. Upon the death of then brewery president Michael Martz, his sons, George and Albert, joined the brewery, with both working as the secretary-treasurer. Frank Martz's son, Charles, was also part of the company. Detroit Brewing Company remained family-

Detroit Brewing Company beer delivery truck. *Courtesy of Atwater Brewery.*

owned for its nearly eighty-year existence. The main beer brands of Detroit Brewing Company were Oldbru, Bohemian, Extra and Erlanger. Oldbru's tagline was, "Scientifically Brewed and Properly Aged." Bohemian's tagline was, "The Great Family Beer."

Detroit Brewing Company's Bohemian beer was in direct competition with Stroh's Bohemian Lager. During Prohibition, the brewery remained closed, but the Martz family remained as owners. The company re-formed in 1934 and started brewing the Oldbru beer brand again. Peak production for Detroit Brewing Company came in 1946 at 211,000 barrels. Sales started to fall at Detroit Brewing Company to 71,000 barrels in 1948. The Martz family attempted to sell the business but had no takers, and the brewery closed in early 1949. Today, the building that once housed Detroit Brewing Company still stands in Eastern Market at the corner of Orleans and Adelaide Streets. It is used for refrigerated meat storage and warehousing under the name of Metro Cold Storage.

Ekhardt & Becker Brewing Company

In 1883, August Ekhardt and Herman Becker purchased the Ulmer Brewery on Russell Street in Detroit. They named their newly purchased brewery the Michigan Brewery. In 1891, they merged with Fulda & Boomer Brewery, which was located on Winder and Orleans Streets in the Eastern Market area of Detroit. In 1891, they moved to the corner of Winder and Orleans Streets, used the larger brewery to expand operations and closed the smaller Michigan Brewery on Russell Street. They continued acquisitions by purchasing the Westphalia Brewery, and eventually they started brewing under the name Ekhardt and Becker Brewing Company. August Ekhardt's son, August Jr., joined the brewery in 1914 as the brewmaster. August Ekhardt and Herman Becker closed the brewery during Prohibition and sold the plant.

After Prohibition, the Ekhardt and Becker Brewing Company was reestablished with new investors and renamed E&B. The sons of one of the original founders, August Becker Jr. and William Becker, were involved in the new brewery formation. E&B acquired the Regal Brewing Company in 1937 and started marketing a "Steinie" beer using the slogan "Flavored with Age" in the early 1940s. Schmidt Brewery was acquired by E&B in 1952. The company was brewing beers under the labels of

E&B Brewing Company site. *Photo by Stephen Johnson.*

E&B beer, E&B Golden Ale and Schmidt beer. E&B's peak production was 244,000 barrels annually.

In 1963, Pfeiffer acquired E&B and formed a new entity called Associated Brewing. It ceased brewing at the E&B brewery site on Winder Street and moved to the larger Pfeiffer Brewery on Bellevue Street on Detroit's lower eastside. The E&B brewhouse and office still stand today. The E&B Brewery Lofts are housed in the historic Ekhardt & Becker Brewery. The building reopened in 1970 with some of the first residential loft spaces in Detroit. The building stands nine stories tall and is the tallest building in the Eastern Market area. In early 2012, the Red Bull House of Art opened up in the E&B Brewery Lofts building. The art gallery is the only one of its kind in North America. Red Bull House of Art supplies eight different local artists with the tools, materials and studio space in the gallery. Every three months, the artists showcase their work to the public.

DETROIT BEER

Zynda Brewing Company

Four Breweries existed in Detroit and Hamtramck to serve the Polish community from 1886 until 1948. Wayne Brewing Company operated from 1933 to 1937, and Thomas Zoltowski Brewery was in business from 1891 to 1919. Auto City Brewing Company was active from 1910 to 1941. And Zynda Brewing Company, which operated from 1886 to 1948, was the most well known of the four breweries.

John Zynda formed the White Eagle Brewery in 1886. He located his small brewery at the corner of Brush and Macomb Streets in what is the Greektown area of Detroit today. In 1891, John Zynda moved his brewery to Canfield and Riopelle Streets just north of Eastern Market. John's brother, Theophilus, joined the company that same year, and they renamed the brewery John Zynda & Brothers. During Prohibition, the company changed its name to John Zynda & Sons to reflect his family joining the company. In order to survive during Prohibition, the company produced soft drinks and near beer. However, rumor has it that the company also continued producing beer. According to Zynda family descendants, a tunnel connected the brewery to a garage across the street. A lookout from the

Crystal Pale beer label. *Photo by Noreen Johnson.*

nearby hardware store would let John Zynda & Sons know when the coast was clear. Then a truck full of real beer would leave the garage headed for local speakeasies in Hamtramck. Due to the political connections that John Zynda Sr. had in the Polish community, the police turned a blind eye toward the illegal activity.

John Zynda Jr. re-formed the company after Prohibition as Zynda Brewing Company in 1933, and peak production was achieved the following year at forty-eight thousand barrels. The main beer brands of Zynda Brewing Company were Zynda's Lager, Crystal Pale and Muenchener. The company closed for good in 1948. A plumbing supply company used the brewery buildings until they were demolished in the 1970s. Today, the site that once housed Zynda Brewing Company is a public city park called Forest Park. It houses a baseball diamond, a basketball court and lots of green space. The park is directly across the street from a large Polish church called Sweetest Heart of Mary Church. Every August, church members throw the largest pierogi festival in Detroit as they celebrate the great history of the Polish people in the Detroit area.

Auto City Brewing Company

Stanislav and Joseph Chronowski formed Auto City Brewing Company in 1910, and they located their brewery in Hamtramck close to the Dodge Main Plant. The brothers tried selling soft drinks and liquid malt during Prohibition. In 1934, the brewery resumed brewing beer. Since yeast absorbs vitamin B during fermentation, Auto City Brewing Company used an exclusive process that restored the vitamin B to the beer and would therefore extol the health benefits of its beer. This was a common sales tactic in the early 1900s. The Food and Drug Administration eventually banned companies from making vitamin-advertising claims for alcoholic beverages. Peak production for Auto City Brewing Company was seventy-five thousand barrels annually in 1936. The beer brands that Auto City Brewing Company marketed were Auto City and Altweiser. Auto City Brewing Company closed for good in 1941. Like many other breweries of its size, it just couldn't compete in the era of regional and national beer brands that were invading the Detroit market.

Auto City beer label. *Photo by Noreen Johnson.*

TIVOLI BREWING COMPANY

Tivoli Brewing Company was founded in 1897 by Frank Brogniez, Bernhard Verstein and Louis Schimmel. All three were part of Detroit's Belgian community. Since Germans started the majority of breweries in Detroit, Tivoli (started by Belgians) was unique in the local Detroit market. The original Tivoli Brewing Company was built on Mack Avenue at the outer edge of Eastern Market in Detroit. It operated at this location from 1897 to 1919.

Tivoli Brewing Company kept the brewery open during Prohibition by producing soft drinks and liquid malt. After Prohibition, Tivoli Brewing Company built a larger brewery at 10205 Mack in the Jefferson-Chalmers area of Detroit. It reopened in 1934 with sales of 154,000 barrels. By 1936, sales at Tivoli Brewing Company had increased to 357,000 barrels. The beer brands that the company marketed were Tivoli Pilsner, Altes Lager, Altes Imperial and Skyball. The Altes brand was so popular that Tivoli Brewing Company renamed itself Altes Brewing Company in 1949.

National Brewing Company out of Baltimore, Maryland, purchased Altes Brewing Company in 1955. National produced the popular beer brand National Bohemian, or "Natty Boh." National Brewing Company

Altes Lager beer label. *Photo by Noreen Johnson.*

of Michigan was then formed, and the Detroit brewery produced the National Bohemian beer. However, sales were not as expected on Natty Boh, and Altes Lager beer was reintroduced to the market. Despite the change, sales continued to slide. The Detroit brewery was closed in 1973, and production was shifted back to Baltimore. Carling Brewery of Canada then spun off its United States division in 1975. The new U.S. company merged with National Brewing Company to become Carling-National Breweries. Carling had originally purchased the Frankenmuth Brewery in Frankenmuth, Michigan, and was producing Carling Black Label from that brewery during 1956–90. Carling-National Brewery was then purchased by G. Heileman of Lacrosse, Wisconsin, in 1979. In 1994, Stroh Brewing Company purchased G. Heileman. Today, Stroh, Black Label and National Bohemian are all owned and marketed by Pabst Brewing Company.

As Detroit and the rest of the country lost the majority of their local and regional breweries in the 1980s and 1990s, a new beer movement was starting to take hold: craft beer. In the next chapters of this book, the

National Bohemian beer label. *Photo by Noreen Johnson.*

craft beer movement will be chronicled—including an explanation of what craft beer is and why Detroit is one of the best markets for craft beer in the United States.

A HISTORY OF BREWING IN THE MOTOR CITY

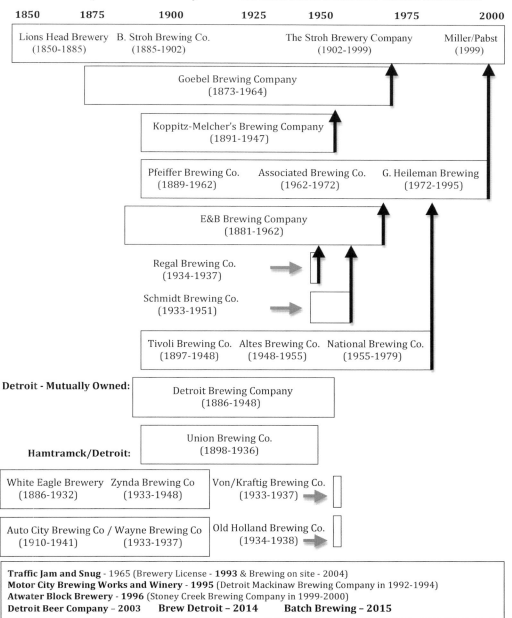

Chart 1 - 1933 (POST PROHIBITION) – 12+ BREWERIES MADE BEER IN DOWNTOWN DETROIT!

1850	1875	1900	1925	1950	1975	2000

Lions Head Brewery (1850-1885) B. Stroh Brewing Co. (1885-1902) The Stroh Brewery Company (1902-1999) Miller/Pabst (1999)

Goebel Brewing Company (1873-1964)

Koppitz-Melcher's Brewing Company (1891-1947)

Pfeiffer Brewing Co. (1889-1962) Associated Brewing Co. (1962-1972) G. Heileman Brewing (1972-1995)

E&B Brewing Company (1881-1962)

Regal Brewing Co. (1934-1937)

Schmidt Brewing Co. (1933-1951)

Tivoli Brewing Co. (1897-1948) Altes Brewing Co. (1948-1955) National Brewing Co. (1955-1979)

Detroit - Mutually Owned: Detroit Brewing Company (1886-1948)

Hamtramck/Detroit: Union Brewing Co. (1898-1936)

White Eagle Brewery (1886-1932) Zynda Brewing Co (1933-1948) Von/Kraftig Brewing Co. (1933-1937)

Auto City Brewing Co / Wayne Brewing Co (1910-1941) (1933-1937) Old Holland Brewing Co. (1934-1938)

Traffic Jam and Snug - 1965 (Brewery License - **1993** & Brewing on site - 2004)
Motor City Brewing Works and Winery - **1995** (Detroit Mackinaw Brewing Company in 1992-1994)
Atwater Block Brewery - **1996** (Stoney Creek Brewing Company in 1999-2000)
Detroit Beer Company – **2003**   **Brew Detroit – 2014**   **Batch Brewing – 2015**

The Craft Beer Movement

1990s-Present

Many would say that the reemergence of breweries and brewpubs in the United States occurred because the public had grown tired of fizzy, light, boring lagers and began to crave flavor and variety. Others might say that the growth of craft beer is the result of the many home brewers and home brew shops and clubs that have started up all across the United States. Both are correct.

By the 1970s, the United States' beer market was composed of little variety and just a few breweries. The United States had gone from nearly 4,000 breweries in the pre-Prohibition era to fewer than 50 that remained in business by 1982. The craft beer renaissance started on the West Coast and was influenced by Fritz Maytag buying the nearly bankrupt Anchor Brewing in 1965. He started selling Anchor Steam Beer in bottles in 1971. Jack McAuliffe opened the New Albion Brewing Company in 1976 and became the first microbrewery of the modern era. These two gentlemen both influenced new generations of brewery owners, from Ken Grossman of Sierra Nevada Brewing to Jim Koch of Boston Beer Company. All of these early beer pioneers broke from the traditional light lagers to bring flavorful beers back to the U.S. market. What started on the West Coast in the early 1970s and 1980s eventually cascaded across the United States. According to the Brewers Association, in 2015 there were 4,144 breweries operating in the United States. That is the highest brewery count since the pre-Prohibition high in 1873 of 4,131 breweries. Craft brewers reached 11 percent volume of the total U.S. beer market and continue to grow share and volume each year.

A HISTORY OF BREWING IN THE MOTOR CITY

On October 14, 1978, President Jimmy Carter signed the law allowing home brewing for personal use and consumption. H.R. 1337 allows U.S. citizens to brew one hundred gallons of beer per year per person or two hundred gallons per household, as long as they do not sell it. Prior to this law, if you produced beer in your home, you were required to pay excise taxes. According to the American Home Brewers Association, there are nearly 1.2 million home brewers in the United States producing more than 2 million barrels of beer a year. That equals 1 percent of the annual output of all of the beer produced in the United States.

What is craft beer? The Brewers Association (the trade group for the craft beer industry) developed the commonly used definition for craft beer: "an American craft brewer is small, independent and traditional." The association further defined terms as follows: "small" means that the annual production is 6 million barrels of beer or less; "independent" means that less than 25 percent of the craft brewery is owned or controlled (or has an equivalent economic interest) by an alcoholic beverage industry member that is not himself a craft brewer; and "traditional" means that a brewer has a majority of its total beverage alcohol volume in beers whose flavor is derived from traditional or innovative brewing ingredients and their fermentation.

There are many that helped spark the craft beer resurgence in Michigan. One was Bell's Beer on the west side of the state. Larry Bell originally opened up a home brew supply shop in 1983. He started selling beer and incorporated under the name Kalamazoo Brewing Company in 1985, the same year that Stroh Brewery Company closed its iconic downtown Detroit brewery. Kalamazoo Brewing Company was officially renamed Bell's Brewery Incorporated in 2006.

Larry Bell and a handful of others helped establish the Michigan Brewers Guild in 1997 with 30 member breweries. The Michigan Brewers Guild is an organization whose goal is to promote Michigan beer, unify Michigan brewers and ensure a healthy beer industry in the state. Today, it is one of the strongest guilds in the nation with more than 160 members.

According to the Michigan Brewers Guild, the beer manufacturing licenses are split up into three types in Michigan: a brewery, a microbrewery and a brewpub license.

- A BREWERY can sell directly to consumers in not more than two of its locations, as well as through retailers across the state. This license is the broadest since there is no restriction on amounts produced or the source of distribution.

- A MICROBREWERY can produce up to sixty thousand barrels annually. It may sell beer for consumption at its location or though retailers across the state. Microbreweries producing thirty thousand to sixty thousand barrels annually are limited to three brewery locations, while microbreweries producing less than thirty thousand barrels annually are not limited in the number of brewery locations.

- A BREWPUB is limited to six locations and can manufacture up to eighteen thousand barrels annually in combined production, and its beer is sold only inside its own establishment. The brewpub must have an "on-premises license" (Class C, Tavern, A-Hotel, B-Hotel or Resort) and may offer a full-service bar. It must also operate a full-service restaurant with at least 25 percent of its gross sales from non-alcoholic items.

Today, the craft beer scene in Michigan is one of the most vibrant in the country. Michigan ranks sixth in the nation for number of breweries (159 according to the 2014 Brewers Association website). Michigan has added another 40 breweries to the state in 2015. Michigan craft brewers produced 825,103 barrels in 2014, ranking it tenth in the nation. Michigan is indeed a great beer state.

People think of Detroit as the Motor City because of its long history with the auto industry, a fact that is often noted when the media mentions Detroit. So, when craft beer history is discussed, most people are quick to mention brewers on the west side of the state. What these people do not realize is that downtown Detroit and the metropolitan area are home to many of the original breweries that opened up in the early 1990s in Michigan. The Detroit Metro area has a long and colorful brewing history. Subsequent chapters of this book will explore the backstories of the original breweries and the new wave of breweries that have opened since 1992.

Downtown Detroit

Traffic Jam and Snug Restaurant & Brewery (511 West Canfield Street, Detroit)

Traffic Jam and Snug is one of the most unique brewpubs in downtown Detroit. It is a brewpub, a dairy, a bakery and a restaurant all rolled into one. It even has its own rooftop garden and employs a gardener to take care of it. In addition to its great lineup of beers, the selection of made-from-scratch food products should put Traffic Jam on everybody's list of must-visit brewpubs.

Traffic Jam and Snug was opened in 1965 by owners Richard Vincent and Ben Edwards. The brewpub's name comes from a commonly told story. A Midtown local was speaking with the original owners and said, "If you ever do any business there [indicating the location], it will be a real traffic jam." The name stuck, and Traffic Jam and Snug has been at the corner of Second and Canfield Streets for more than fifty years now. (A bit of trivia: a "snug" was a small, private room located in an English or Irish pub. The room had bar access, and any glass windows were placed above head height. Patrons paid a bit more for beer in the snug, but they could enjoy the beverages unobserved by others.)

In 1992, the former Traffic Jam and Snug attorney and friend Tom Burns helped get the law changed in Michigan that allows brewpubs. Prior to the change, restaurants were not allowed to operate with an on-site brewery.

Traffic Jam and Snug became the first licensed brewpub in Michigan in 1992. However, because of the wording of the brewpub law, Traffic Jam and Snug was unable to hold a liquor license and a brewery license at the same time. To solve the problem, Tom Burns went across the street from Traffic Jam and opened the Detroit Mackinaw Brewing Company in 1992, and that is where Traffic Jam and Snug had its wort contract-brewed until 2001. Wort is the liquid extracted from the mashing process during the brewing of beer. Wort contains the sugars that will be fermented by the brewing yeast to produce alcohol.

Unfortunately, Tom Burns lost his battle with cancer in 1994, and the brewery had to be closed. Tom's original brewer, John Lindardos, reopened the Detroit Mackinaw Brewing Company, renaming it Motor City Brewing Works and Winery later that year.

Carolyn Howard and her husband, Scott Lowell, bought Traffic Jam and Snug in 1999 when the founders retired. In 2001, Traffic Jam started making its own beer when the owners hired Chris Reilly to be its head brewer and cheesemaker. Chris Reilly was a home brewer, but he had never brewed professionally—nor had he ever made cheese. With the help of friend and brewer Greg Burke, Chris learned how to use Traffic Jam's dual-use dairy and brewing equipment. Scott Lowell had learned how to make cheese from the original owners, and he had earned his cheesemaker's license in Wisconsin. Scott taught Reilly how to make cheese using the dual-use equipment. Traffic Jam's beer was brewed and open-fermented on the same equipment that was used to make cheese.

Of course, the challenge with running the dual operation was that if someone was making cheese, someone else couldn't be making beer and vice-versa. Traffic Jam and Snug's cheese and beer production increased to the point that sharing equipment was no longer plausible. Today, there is a dedicated brewing system and separate dedicated dairy equipment. Traffic Jam averages more than two hundred barrels annually on the current brew system and typically has five beers on draft in the brewpub. Traffic Jam and Snug was the first restaurant in the state of Michigan to be licensed by the Department of Agriculture as a licensed dairy. Traffic Jam and Snug exclusively purchases all its milk used for cheese production through Cook's Farm Dairy in Ortonville, Michigan. By using one dairy farm for all its milk, Traffic Jam can ensure that both it and Cook's Farm Dairy have followed all of the Michigan Department of Agriculture rules and regulations. The cheese that Traffic Jam and Snug produces is made in five-hundred-gallon vats

Traffic Jam and Snug beer list. *Photo by Stephen Johnson.*

that yield 480 pounds of cheese. The brewpub sells its cheese in the restaurant and also at select local retailers.

Chris Reilly was the head brewer and cheese maker from 2001 to 2014. Today, the owners are shaking things up at Traffic Jam and Snug with a new generation of brewers. These new brewers continue the traditions of making both cheese and beer. However, they are experimenting with some new ideas and beer recipes to add to Traffic Jam and Snug's regular lineup. Besides producing the great standard beers of pilsner, India pale ale and maibock, they are bringing interesting new twists on older beer styles such as dinkel, a beer made from an ancient grain called splet, which was a precursor to wheat. Prior to wheat being the industrialized crop we have today, splet was commonly used in Europe.

Since 2011, Traffic Jam and Snug has donated the use of its parking lot for the staging area of the annual Marche du Nain Rouge, which draws thousands of spectators each year. Marche du Nain Rouge is part Mardi Gras celebration with bands and music and part parade with floats and people in wild costumes. The event celebrates the banishing of the Nain Rouge, which is a Detroit

Traffic Jam and Snug exterior. *Photo by Stephen Johnson.*

urban legend. The Nain Rouge, or "Red Dwarf," is a mythical creature that supposedly appears prior to terrible events in the city. For example, it has been said that in 1701, the creature attacked the first white settler of Detroit, Antoine Cadillac, and after the altercation, Cadillac soon lost his fortune. Today, the parade leaves Traffic Jam and Snug and goes down Second Avenue to Cass Park. At the conclusion of the parade, the Red Dwarf is banished from the city for another year. Fiction author Josef Bastian wrote a trilogy book series with the Nain Rouge as the main character.

Traffic Jam and Snug owners Carolyn Howard and Scott Lowell are involved in many activities in the Midtown community that extend beyond the restaurant and brewery. They have also helped restore and develop multiple homes in the area. In 2003, they renovated the Blackstone on Second Avenue. The home and area around it were known for illegal activities, and the renovation helped to clean up the area and eliminate the illicit activity. Maybe the most ambitious renovation project to date is the Forest Arms, located at Second Avenue and Prentis Street. The building dates from 1908 and is a gateway building into the neighborhood. The building burned in 1989 and had been left in rough shape prior to the renovation. The seventy-unit building is set to open in November 2015 and will add much-needed one- and two-bedroom apartments to the neighborhood. These projects helped improve the area, which in turn drew new businesses to the neighborhood and inspired the owners to build an outdoor seating area for its customers.

In August 2015, Traffic Jam and Snug celebrated its fiftieth anniversary with a daylong celebration that included a special dubbel beer and blue asiago cheese release. Carolyn Howard stated, "We are most proud of our role in the community. Through the longevity of being open fifty years, we have had multigenerational customers and regulars." They have provided stability on the corner of Second Avenue and Canfield in Midtown. With the Midtown area becoming increasingly popular, Traffic Jam and Snug will continue to be a popular destination for beer and foodies alike.

MOTOR CITY BREWING WORKS
(470 WEST CANFIELD STREET, DETROIT)

Motor City Brewing Works is the oldest operating brewery in Detroit and is located directly across the street from Traffic Jam and Snug, the first brewpub in Michigan. The building that today houses Motor City Brewing Works was once home to Detroit and Mackinaw Brewing Company from 1992 to 1994. As noted previously, it originally opened to produce beer for Traffic Jam and Snug across the street. John Linardos, who grew up in the same area as the brewery, was one of the original brewers there. In 1994, John took over the brewery, renamed it Motor City Brewing Works and produced and sold his first draft beer there in 1995. What today is called the Midtown

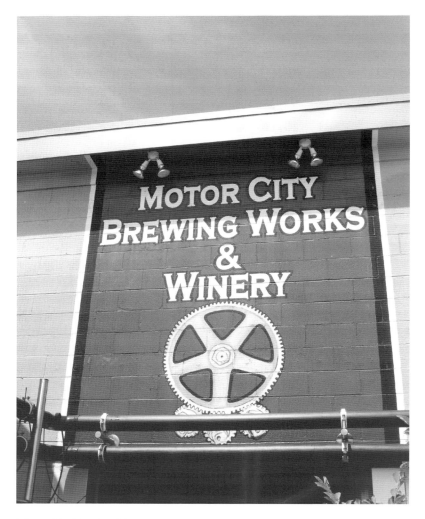

Motor City Brewing Works & Winery sign. *Photo by Stephen Johnson.*

area had originally been considered the Cass Corridor neighborhood of Detroit. When the brewery originally opened, the Cass Corridor area was a community of artists, musicians and activists. Today, this area has been transformed into one of the hottest areas to live in downtown Detroit. It is nestled between Wayne State University, Detroit Medical Center, Detroit Institute of Arts and the soon-to-be new arena district, which will be the home to the Detroit Red Wings. Motor City Brewing Works is right in the center of all of this growth and prosperity.

A HISTORY OF BREWING IN THE MOTOR CITY

Motor City Brewing Works originally produced beer on site for sale to distributors of draft beer only. A bottling line was added in 1998, and eventually a taproom was opened to the public in 2001. In 2007, a wood-fired oven and kitchen was built to make pizzas for hungry customers. In 2011, Motor City Brewing Works replaced its aging bottling line with a new custom bottling line made in Italy. This addition increased its needed bottling capacity. In 2014, it added additional fermenters. Motor City Brewing Works brews on a ten-barrel system and produces three thousand barrels of beer annually. In 2015, it began working with a local contract brewery in Corktown called Brew Detroit to brew and can Ghettoblaster, Motor City Brewing Works' Detroit-style mild ale and flagship beer. Contracting out its most popular beer allows Motor City Brewing Works to free up capacity at its brewery to experiment on new beer styles and grow its business without the added cost of building a larger brewhouse.

Motor City Brewing Works' head brewer and co-owner is Dan Scarsella. He leads a team of three other brewers: Robert Schmidt, Charlie McCutcheon and Mike Pierce. Dan has a diverse brewing background that includes brewing for Great Baraboo Brewing in Clinton Township from 1994 to 1995, Harpers Brewpub in East Lansing from 1995 to 1997 and CJ's Brewery in Commerce Township from 1997 to 2006. All of these previous breweries provided a great environment for Dan to learn more about the brewing process. In the early 1990s, there were few brewers in the state of Michigan, so the people who were brewing at that time were constantly helping and learning from other brewers in the industry. It was a much smaller community back then compared to the more vibrant and growing craft scene of today.

In 2010, Motor City Brewing Works, with the help of local community partners, transformed the alley behind the brewery into the Green Alley. The alley was closed off to vehicular traffic and transformed into a more pedestrian-friendly area. The alley had been a trash- and graffiti-ridden alley typical of many alleyways in the city of Detroit. The nearly two-year-long project created an earth-friendly patch of permeable asphalt that recycles water to nurture native plants and is lighted by energy-efficient streetlamps. In 2015, Motor City Brewing Works converted the space in front of the brewery into outdoor seating and six permeable asphalt parking spots with planters in front of them. This addition added another attractive feature to an already thoughtfully designed brewhouse and taproom.

John Linardos has always supported his artistic roots with Motor City Brewing Works. Ghettoblaster, its flagship Detroit-style mild ale, is also the name of a series of music recordings. "Beer You Can Hear" is the tagline on the bottles and cans. The two *Ghettoblaster* albums that have been released are for sale in the brewery or online through the website. According to the website, the original *Ghettoblaster* music sampler was recorded in 1997 and featured the Dirtbombs, the Witches, Kim Fowley, Outrageous Cherry and many other artists. A second volume soon followed featuring more local Detroit artists. A third volume is currently in the works. "*Ghettoblaster* was born during a great Cass Corridor time when it was full of underground music and art," Linardos said.

"This Week in Art" occurs every Wednesday at the brewery. Originally, it was started four years ago by Graem White and is now organized by Amy Abbott. Each week, a single artist installs an exhibition in the intimate space inside the brewery.

In the spring of 2015, Motor City Brewing Works began brewing Le Rouge Ale, the official craft beer of Detroit City FC, Detroit's minor-league soccer team. The ale is a cross between the brewery's popular Bohemian Lager and a red ale. Le Rouge is a light and malty beer that can be enjoyed both on and off the soccer field. In addition to Le Rouge and Ghettoblaster, Motor City Brewing Works' standard beers include a nut brown ale, a honey porter, an India pale ale, a pale ale and a hard cider. It offers a rotating list of seasonal beers that include Summer Brew, Corktown Stout, Oktoberfest and a pumpkin ale.

Motor City Brewing Works celebrated its twentieth anniversary with what it called "Canniversary" on August 1, 2015. The event was held at New Center Park just north of the brewery and featured live music, food and plenty of beer. It also showcased the release of Ghettoblaster in cans. Detroit's well-known pop artist Glenn Barr designed the artwork for the can and the fifteen-pack case. Selling Ghettoblaster in a can makes the beer more shelf stable, and therefore it can travel longer distances. This will, in turn, expand Motor City Brewing Works' beer beyond its traditional Michigan markets.

Motor City Brewing Works began in a small rented building that supplied beer to local bars and wort to Traffic Jam and Snug. Eventually, it became a model of a community-based brewery that not only supports the area around it but also produces great beers that are enjoyed all over Detroit.

A HISTORY OF BREWING IN THE MOTOR CITY

DETROIT BEER COMPANY (1529 BROADWAY STREET, DETROIT)

Detroit Beer Company opened in 2003, and at the time of its opening, it was part of a trio of local brewpubs owned by Beercos, which had been started by Drew Ciora and Mike Plesz. The two other brewpubs were Royal Oak Brewery, which opened in 1995, and Rochester Mills Beer Company, which opened in 1998. The two partners split up Beercos into two separate companies in 2008, when they both wanted to develop other brewery and restaurant concepts. Drew Ciora kept Royal Oak Brewery and Detroit Beer Company, and Mike Plesz kept Rochester Mills Beer Company. In 2010, Drew went on to open Lockhart's BBQ in Royal Oak and added a Lake Orion location in 2015. The Royal Oak location is located across the parking lot from Royal Oak Brewery.

The Detroit Beer Company renovated the historical Hartz Building at a cost of $5.3 million. The Hartz Building was an early twentieth-century surgical supply store and was renovated to accommodate a restaurant, brewery equipment and office space. The brewhouse and fermentation tanks are housed in the basement, while serving tanks are positioned directly behind the main bar. Detroit Beer Company offers many standard and seasonal beers. The standard beers include Detroit Lager, Local 1529 IPA, People Mover Porter and Detroit Dwarf. Throughout the course of the year, it also offers many seasonal offerings that include Baseball Beer, Double Dwarf, Hockeytown Hefeweizen, Riopelle Rye Pale Ale and Belgian Dark Strong Ale to name a few. Detroit Beer Company produces an average of 850 barrels per year from its custom basement brewhouse. Current head brewer Justin Riopelle continues to offer beer lovers a great selection of craft beers.

One of the flagship beers is Detroit Dwarf, a German alt-style beer named in reference to the Nain Rouge, the mythical creature described in the Traffic Jam and Snug section. Over the years, the tales about the Red Dwarf have continued to be told and retold. Thus, Detroit Beer Company honors this aspect of Detroit's history with the name of this beer.

Detroit Beer Company is located near Comerica Park and Ford Field and across the street from the Detroit Opera House. Its unique location ensures plenty of traffic during major sporting and cultural events in the city. It has great beer and food, and it's a great place to watch sports in the D.

DETROIT BEER

JOLLY PUMPKIN PIZZERIA & BREWERY DETROIT
(441 WEST CANFIELD STREET, DETROIT)

Jolly Pumpkin Pizzeria & Brewery Detroit is the most recent beer destination to open in downtown Detroit. It opened its doors to the public in April 2015. Jolly Pumpkin Pizzeria & Brewery Detroit is the third café location in the expanding portfolio of properties with the Jolly Pumpkin brand attached to it. It also has café locations in Ann Arbor and Traverse City. Jolly Pumpkin is based in Dexter. The Dexter location is the main production brewery with a tap house attached to it called NULL. The Detroit location does not brew beer on site, but it is included here due to its unique story about sour beer.

Ron Jefferies started Jolly Pumpkin Artisan Ales in 2004 with the goal of producing world-class sour beers. Sour beers are some of the most complex beer styles to produce and are brewed with wild yeast cultures. Jolly Pumpkin Artisan Ales was a trailblazer in the production of sour beers in the United States. Prior to Jolly Pumpkin, U.S. brewers didn't produce any sour beers. They had been more common in Europe, specifically Belgium, but sour beers were virtually nonexistent in the United States until Ron started brewing them.

According to the Jolly Pumpkin Artisan Ales website, the company name developed one afternoon when Ron Jefferies and his wife were on their porch sipping a beer and brainstorming about what to call their brewery. This quote from the website describes it best:

Many great names came forth that afternoon, but as the weeks passed, and spring finally sprung, the name that always made us smile was Jolly Pumpkin. It encompassed everything we wanted to express about our brewery. Fun and quirky, all that needed adding were the last two words; "Artisan Ales," the description of the brewery's products and mission; The creation of fantastic beers of truly outstanding artisan quality. Maintaining traditional small-scale production, keeping beer a beverage of both outstanding complexity and simplicity, this would be our laudable goal. Complexity of flavor, simplicity of ingredient and process. This duality was perfectly balanced in the name. Simple and complex. Complex yet simple.

Jolly Pumpkin Pizzeria & Brewery Detroit has thirty-two beers on tap at any given time. It also serves some pretty tasty pizza and has outdoor seating available to guests. Part of the appeal of Jolly Pumpkin Pizzeria

& Brewery is that it not only serves Jolly Pumpkin beers, but this location also serves North Peak and Grizzly Peak brands. All three of the beer brands are part of Northern United Brewing Company—NUBCo for short, the retail distribution part of this company. Under NUBCo, it also produces Bonafide Wines, Old Mission Micro and Civilized Spirits, all of which are served there.

Another side of NUBCo is developing unique properties. Jon Carlson and Greg Lobdell started Two Mission Design and Development. Their first development was in Ann Arbor in 1994. They focus on multiuse and urban locations typically at historically significant properties. Besides the Jolly Pumpkin properties, the duo has developed North Peak Brewery in Traverse City, Grizzly Peak Brewery and Blue Tractor BBQ and Brewery in Ann Arbor and Bastone Brewery in Royal Oak, as well as many other restaurant, bar and club concepts.

The opportunity to drink a large variety of sour beers in one location is what really sets Jolly Pumpkin Pizzeria & Brewery Detroit apart from other breweries and bars in downtown Detroit. On any given visit, about a dozen of the taps are Jolly Pumpkin beers. In a time when multi-tap beer bars are opening up all over the Detroit area, beer drinkers would be hard pressed to find any that would have that large a selection of sour beers on draft all the time.

BATCH BREWING COMPANY (1400 PORTER STREET, DETROIT)

Batch Brewing Company opened its doors in February 2015 on the same weekend as its Corktown neighbor, Brew Detroit. Batch Brewing Company is downtown Detroit's first nanobrewery. A nanobrewery means brewing is done in small batches, and there is not typically a standard beer lineup. In the case of Batch Brewing Company, a four-barrel system is used during the brewing process, which yields about eight kegs of beer. Its focus is on producing clean and fresh beers for an ever-changing list of more than ten beers on draft.

Stephen Roginson and Jason Williams started Batch Brewing Company with the $50,000 they were awarded in the Hatch Detroit Competition and also raised an additional $25,000 through a successful Indiegogo campaign. They added head cellar man Patrick Ahrens (formerly of Motor City Brewing Works) and head chef Matt Johnson (a sixteen-year restaurant veteran) to create an experienced team of people that keeps the small brewery running smoothly.

The open layout of Batch Brewing Company is part of its appeal to customers. You can see the majority of the brewing operation from the four large communal tables and the long row of bar seats in the taproom. The building that once housed the Porter Street Station Bar & Grill is nearly four thousand square feet in size, can seat seventy people inside and offers additional outside seating. Although the original business plan was to not offer food, there was already a kitchen installed by the former building tenants. Consequently, Batch Brewing Company decided to make use of it and began offering a limited menu of rotating dishes that complement the beer list.

Batch Brewing also has acquired a unique feature to the building: a boxcar that was left over from the former tenants and has a giant Batch Brewing Company logo painted on it. Patrons cannot miss it as they pull up to the brewery. Another distinguishing feature at Batch Brewing Company is the Feelgood Tap. Once a month, Batch Brewing Company partners with a local charity or nonprofit group. Two dollars from each pint sold from the Feelgood Tap goes to that charity. According to Batch Brewing Company's website, "We're convinced we'll be able to be wildly successful AND make a positive impact on the community around us. We create a beer to honor that partner. Then, we sell it to you. It's pretty simple: drink good beer and do some good!" It's a program that has already raised thousands of dollars for multiple nonprofits in the Detroit area. It shows the community-based focus that Batch Brewing Company brings to the Corktown neighborhood.

Having two vastly different-sized breweries within a one-block walk from each other makes Batch Brewing Company and Brew Detroit great stops for any beer enthusiast looking to check out the Corktown area of downtown Detroit.

Brew Detroit (1401 Abbott Street, Detroit)

Opened in 2014, Brew Detroit is located in a sixty-eight-thousand-square-foot industrial building in the Corktown area of Detroit. The building is the former Detroit Ball Bearing Building, and Brew Detroit employs about thirty people. It is a contract brewery that brews, bottles, cans and kegs for other breweries. A contract brewery is a brewery that brews someone else's beer under contract. The practice is not new in the United States, but it is new to downtown Detroit. Brew Detroit has invested $10 million to build a modern brewery capable of brewing seventy thousand barrels of beer on its one-hundred-barrel BrauKon brew system and towering four-hundred-barrel fermentation tanks. The system is fully automated, which helps the staff maintain the character of each brewery's beers. A small on-site laboratory tests each batch to match the flavor, color and consistency for each brewery.

Brew Detroit is currently brewing beer under contracts with Atwater Brewery, Motor City Brewing Works and KR Drinks LLC (Kid Rock's Badass American Lager), with more breweries to follow. Mark Rieth, owner of Atwater Brewery, is one of the minority owners of Brew Detroit. The original principal investors of Brew Detroit were Keith Sorois and David Crawford from Big Boy Restaurants and Don Foss, owner of Credit Acceptance Corporation. Additional investors have been added to the operation since its inception.

An obvious advantage of contracting out your beer is that a brewery owner doesn't need to invest in the added equipment and expense at his/her own brewery. For many breweries in Michigan and the rest of the country, capacity and access to capital are major roadblocks to growing beer brands beyond their current breweries or brewpubs. By contracting with Brew Detroit, John Linardos, the owner and founder of Motor City Brewing Works, said, "He's been able to double his production without building another factory of his own." With the Brew Detroit owners having anchor contracts in place by some well-established brewery names, they were able to secure the financing to get Brew Detroit off the ground.

Brew Detroit has built a well-oiled beer-producing machine that is a welcome addition to the downtown Detroit brewery scene. It added extra brewing capacity to a growing craft beer community in Michigan that is eager to expand its beers outside of its brewery's walls.

ATWATER BREWERY
(237 JOSEPH CAMPAU STREET, DETROIT)
AND ATWATER IN THE PARK
(1175 LAKEPOINTE STREET, GROSSE POINTE PARK, MICHIGAN)

Atwater Block Brewery was founded in 1997 in the Warehouse/Rivertown district of Detroit. The brewery is housed in a former automotive parts manufacturing warehouse that was built in 1919. The original crane from the plant is still visible as patrons enter the brewery. Atwater Block Brewery's original owners imported a twenty-barrel Kasper Schultz brew system from Germany. They even hired Germans to consult and help set up the system. The original beer recipes developed at the brewery were all traditional German lagers. According to the website, "Our imported Kasper Schultz brew house allows us to brew our brands in the true heritage-style of traditional German lagers. And, when we say, 'imported brew house,' we mean it! All of our main brewing equipment was brought in from Germany, where precision and passion for beer has its roots. In fact, when we have service calls on our equipment, we call in the Germans!"

New owners came into the brewery in 2001 and renamed it Stoney Creek Brewing Company, a company that had contracted out its beers in the local market. However, the owners decided that Atwater Block Brewery location was a good business opportunity and started brewing beers on their own. Stoney Creek Brewing Company lasted until 2004, when it closed.

In 2002, Mark Rieth became an investor in Stoney Creek Brewing, and in 2005, he bought the brewery outright and changed the name back to Atwater Block Brewery. Today, the name has been shortened to Atwater Brewery. Mark Rieth is a Detroit-area native and Michigan State University alumnus who worked in the automotive industry before moving back to Michigan. Mark was a home brewer and regularly stopped by the former Atwater Block Brewery to drink. When the opportunity came up to purchase the brewery, he jumped at the chance.

Atwater Brewery originally had a taproom that faced Jos Campau Street and a production brewery in the rear of the building. The taproom offered a full bar with all of Atwater's beers on draft and a full menu of food. The taproom closed in 2010 to focus on just brewing beer. When the taproom closed, Atwater offered a small selection of its beer on draft inside the production brewery itself. The space is now called the "Bier Stube." Roughly translated, it's a German term for a room, bar or tavern used primarily for the serving of beer. On any given weekend, the Bier Stube attracts locals and tourists alike wanting to experience a more behind-the-scenes look at a production brewery while enjoying a pint. In 2015, Atwater Brewery reopened its original taproom. The space was remodeled to include the longest bar in Detroit. Part of the remodeled space also includes a kitchen, a distillery and additional brewing equipment.

Atwater Brewery has launched a number of additional expansion projects to increase its brewing capacity. The original brewery on Jos

Campau has undergone a multimillion-dollar expansion adding new tanks, and the current plan is to expand the brewery onto the property directly behind the brewery. Between the original location and the beer it has contract-brewed by Brew Detroit in Corktown, Atwater Brewery will have the capacity to produce 150,000 barrels of beer. Considering it brewed 40,000 barrels in 2014 and 55,000 barrels in 2015, this is a considerable increase in brewing capability. Atwater's expansion plans don't stop at the brewery in Detroit, as it is currently in the middle of building a production brewery in Austin, Texas, that is set to be online by the end of 2016. According to an interview with Model D Media, Atwater Brewery also has plans for another production brewery in the North. Atwater Brewery hopes to enter Canadian markets next year, along with Colorado, California, New York and New Jersey. Its goal is to hit 300,000 barrels of production within five years. It is an exciting time to be on the team at Atwater Brewery.

Atwater's standard beers include Vanilla Java Porter, Dirty Blonde, Grand Circus IPA, Atwater Lager, Purple Gang Pilsner, D-Light Kolsch, Dunkel, Decadent Dark Chocolate Ale, Detroit Pale Ale, Hop-A-Peel and Voodoo Vator Dopplebock. The seasonal beers include Summer Ale, Cherry Wheat, Maibock, Cherry Stout, Bloktober and Winter Bock. Its products are sold in bottles, cans and draft in more than twenty-five states in the United States and soon to be in Canada.

Atwater in the Park opened in 2014 and is housed in the former Grace United Church on the corner of Kerchival and Lakepointe Streets in Grosse Pointe Park. Atwater in the Park is a partnership between the Epicurean Group and Atwater Brewery. The Epicurean Group manages the restaurant side of Atwater in the Park, and Atwater Brewery manages the beer, cider and spirits portion of the business.

Atwater in the Park offers a full lineup of Atwater Brewery beers and authentic German cuisine. It has a small on-site brewhouse creating exclusive beers by head brewer Brad Etheridge. Atwater in the Park also features many of Atwater Brewery's standard beers from the main brewery on Jos Campau. It currently has more than forty beers on tap, with ten being made on site. Atwater in the Park seats 120 people inside the brewery and another 70 outside in its German-style biergarten. Due to the success of Atwater in the Park, the ownership group of Atwater Brewery and the Epicurean Group plan to open up another location in Grand Rapids. They will further expand the Atwater Brand to the west side of the state and bring some of the Detroit grit and hard work with them.

Atwater Brewery has been working hard to expand its product offerings as well. With the recent addition of a distillery, it launched Atwater Spirits and has plans for a hard cider down the road. The spirits are available at its sister property, Atwater in the Park. Atwater Brewery also launched a unique partnership with McClure's, a local Detroit-area business that makes pickles, snack foods and Bloody Mary mix. A combination of Atwater's lager with McClure's Bloody Mary spices makes Michelada (a new beer), and the resulting product is sold in four packs of sixteen-ounce cans in the Detroit area. It has been a great partnership between the two Detroit companies, and Atwater and McClure's are hoping to produce additional products together in the coming years.

Atwater Brewery hosts several annual events at the brewery on Jos Campau. For example, it hosts a series of running events, including Growler Gallop and Hightail to Ale. Both events draw thousands of attendees and help support a local charity. In 2015, Atwater formed its own running club. Members leave from the Jos Campau brewery weekly and finish back at the brewery for a pint or two. Additionally, every fall, Atwater Brewery hosts a Bloktoberfest celebration, which draws more than one thousand people and coincides with its Bloktoberfest beer release.

Atwater Brewery's slogan provides a look into its brewing philosophy: "We drink all we can and sell the rest." As the largest and fastest growing of the downtown Detroit breweries, Atwater Brewery is helping to put Detroit beer on the map in Michigan and in the rest of country.

DOWNRIVER AREA

The rock band Journey would like us to think that there is a South Detroit. In Journey's famous song from 1981, "Don't Stop Believin'," they sing about being born and raised in South Detroit. Through later interviews, Steve Perry, the band's lead singer, admitted that they just made that up. The band and Steve Perry were from the Bay area of California. People from Detroit know that there is not really a South Detroit. On a map, Windsor, Canada, is south of Detroit. However, Downriver is an unofficial name for the region composed of eighteen suburban cities and townships in Wayne County, south of Detroit along the western shore of the Detroit River. These communities are full of the hardworking folks the band Journey referenced in their famous lyrics.

FORT STREET BREWERY (1660 FORTH STREET, LINCOLN PARK)

Pete Romain started Fort Street Brewery in 2005. He has invested a lot of time, money and sweat equity into making Fort Street Brewery a craft beer lover's destination in the Downriver area.

According to Fort Street Brewery's website, the brewery was built new from the ground up on the site of the former Norton's Drug Store. Fort Street Brewery offers affordable food and drinks in a clean and comfortable environment, including many weekly food and drink specials for customer enjoyment. A unique event that the brewery offers is a weekly cask beer tapping. Cask ale is unfiltered, unpasteurized and naturally carbonated beer. The majority of draft beer is served using forced carbonation with either nitrogen or carbon dioxide pressure. Cask ale is popular in Europe, but it has recently had a renaissance here in the United States.

Ryan Walker now runs the brewing duties at Fort Street Brewery. Ryan replaced the longtime brewer, Doug Beedy, who left Fort Street Brewery to open up Tilted Axis Brewing Company in Lapeer. Ryan Walker had previously worked as the assistant brewer at 51 North Brewing in Lake Orion and Granite City Brewery in Troy. Ryan brings a new perspective to the brewery, and it will be exciting to see what he does there. Fort Street Brewery has a fourteen-barrel brewhouse and typically produces six hundred barrels of beer annually.

Sports Brewpub (166 Maple Street, Wyandotte)

Established in 1990 as a bar and grill with a sports and 1950s theme, Sports is today a brewpub with eight handcrafted beers brewed on the premises. Sports Brewpub is Wyandotte's only brewery and offers standard beers including blonde ale, wheat ale, cherry ale, red ale, stout and IPA. One or two seasonal beers are rotated in to change the selection offered, and a full bar is also available. Sports Brewpub fits well in the neighborhood that surrounds it. It offers customers the opportunity to enjoy beer, food and sports. The food menu is varied with bar-type foods, including salads, soups, burgers, sandwiches, pizza, pasta and some pretty good fish tacos.

Eastside and Northeast Side of Metro Detroit

When a local Detroit-area resident asks you in what end of town you reside in Detroit, you might simply answer the eastside or the westside. Where is the dividing line for the east and west sides of the Metro Detroit area? The answers vary, but for the purposes of this book, Woodward Avenue will be it. Some of the most popular breweries in the metropolitan area reside on the east and northeast sides of town. The eastside has some of the earliest breweries and brewpubs that opened in the modern era of craft beer, and some of those breweries have been in business fifteen to twenty years. A lot of great beer started and continues to be made on this end of town. The current wave of new breweries owes a lot to these early craft beer pioneers.

Dragonmead Microbrewery
(14600 East 11 Mile Road, Warren)

If you like Dungeons and Dragons and a large variety of craft beers on tap, then Dragonmead Microbrewery in Warren is the place to visit. Larry Channel, Bill Wrobel and Earl Scherbarth founded Dragonmead Microbrewery in January 1997. The three gentlemen have automotive backgrounds that have helped them design a unique production brewery and taproom. Larry is a Chrysler retiree; Bill currently works at Chrysler;

and Bill's father-in-law, Earl, has retired from Ford. All three started out as home brewers. Eventually, they turned their brewing hobby into a business and launched this very popular Warren microbrewery.

Part of the appeal at Dragonmead Microbrewery is its amazing assortment of beer, wine, cider and mead, all of which are produced on site. Most breweries and brewpubs specialize in Belgian-, American- or German-style beers, but that wasn't good enough for Dragonmead Microbrewery. At any given time, customers can sample from a beer list containing more than forty beers on draft that are listed on the beer menu by country of origin. Patrons can enjoy American-, Belgian-, German-, English-, Russian- and Scottish-style ales and lagers in the taproom. Dragonmead produces these beers true to each respective style and country of origin. The owners even store separate yeast strains, grains and hops that are actually imported from each country of the particular beer style being brewed. Dragonmead eventually wants to have every recognized beer style on draft when customers visit the taproom. Additionally, Dragonmead carries six different meads, twelve different wines and a hard cider. Whatever one's drink of choice, Dragonmead Microbrewery has it covered.

The microbrewery has nearly doubled in space at the Warren location since its humble beginnings in 1997. It now uses nearly eleven thousand square feet of an industrial building on 11 Mile Road in Warren. In 2013, the largest addition to date was completed with the addition of a new twenty-barrel fully automated brew system from Lake Orion–based Craftwerk Brewing Systems. Dragonmead uses the added capacity to brew its flagship beers of Final Absolution, Erik the Red and Under the Kilt Wee Heavy. The expansion has freed up space for Dragonmead to experiment with new recipes on the original 3-barrel system and offer more seasonal beers. In 2015, it produced 2,700 barrels of beer, but with the new system now fully functional, Dragonmead will be able to produce up to 10,000 barrels in the future.

The next time you are on the eastside of Detroit, visit Dragonmead. The variety of beer, mead and wine makes people want to return for more.

Kuhnhenn Brewing Company (5919 Chicago Road, Warren)

Eric Kuhnhenn Sr. started Lutz Hardware in the 1970s. The hardware store catered to the local community in the village of Warren and was located at the corner of Chicago and Mound Roads. Eric Kuhnhenn's sons, Eric Jr.

and Brett, took over the hardware store operations in the early 1990s. They had previously developed an interest in home brewing, and eventually, the brothers started selling home brew supplies out of a section of the hardware store. The home brew supplies started selling better than many of the hardware products and eventually overtook the store. Eric and Brett opened Kuhnhenn Brewing Company in 1998, and what started as only a home brew supply store eventually morphed into a full-scale brewery and home brew supply store in 2001.

The building that once housed Lutz Hardware along with the Sports Shop sporting goods store and Auto Haus Auto Repair Shop is now Kuhnhenn Brewing Company. In 2009, Kuhnhenn Brewing Company moved the home brew shop, Brewing World, across the parking lot into a separate building. Then in 2011, the brewing company took over the space that contained the auto repair shop. Kuhnhenn Brewing Company has retail and draft distribution of its products in Michigan and select parts of New York City and Europe. It currently brews about 2,300 barrels per year.

Kuhnhenn originally started out its operations with a unique feature: a brew-on-premise (BOP) system. This BOP system allowed customers to come in and brew their own batch of beer. Customers went through the entire brew process, from picking out the ingredients and beer recipe to designing a beer label and bottling the product. It was a very popular service. As the brewery grew, so did the need for additional production space. The BOP space was given up in 2011 to expand the brewhouse.

Standard beers at Kuhnhenn Brewing Company include Simcoe Silly, DRIPA (Gold Medal: IPA; 2012 World Beer Cup), Fluffer, Penetration Porter, White Devil, Fest Bier, Loonie Kuhnie Pale Ale, Sully's Kolsch, Imperial Crème Brule Java Stout, and it also produces many seasonal and special bottle releases. Kuhnhenn has won multiple awards and garnered thousands of fans of its beer. With a slogan of "Beers with distinct personalities, since 1998," Kuhnhenn offers an amazing variety for the whole family.

Beer is not the only thing being produced at Kuhnhenn Brewing Company. It serves hard cider and also produces mead and wine. Hard cider is a fermented apple, wine is a fermented grape and mead is a fermented honey. Mead is considered the oldest fermented beverage, and some mead recipes date back more than ten thousand years. A mazer is a person who makes mead. Frank Retell heads the mead-making program at the brewery. He has won numerous local, national and international awards for his meads. Frank is considered the most-awarded mazer in the world. With Kuhnhenn Brewing Company offering wine and mead, it has brought in a more diverse crowd to the brewery. Kuhnhenn offers drinkers a full spectrum of tastes.

According to Skip Pappas (a member of the management team at Kuhnhenn Brewing Company), the Brewing World home brew shop business continues to grow each year. As more people get into craft beer, they become more interested in making it themselves. The consumer continues to mature and crave new tastes and experiences. Home brewing helps provide that creative outlet for craft beer fans to branch out and try new things. By Kuhnhenn Brewing Company having both a taproom and home brew supply store, it benefits from a lot of cross selling between both outlets. For example, a customer could come into the taproom and try a new beer style, and then that customer could walk across the parking lot and talk to someone in the home brew shop about how he/she could make that beer for himself/herself.

Skip Pappas started the Kuhnhenn Guild of Brewers in 2006 to help get more recognition for the brewing industry. According to the home brew club's website, it strives to promote the responsible appreciation of the brewing arts, provide a forum for learning and generally advance the understanding of beer and brewing to not only club members but to the general public as well. The club has more than sixty paid members and is a regular fixture at all Kuhnhenn Brewing Company events. It meets the first Monday of every month at the brewery. The club hosts special brew events for National Homebrew Day in May and a chili cook-off in November each year.

Kuhnhenn has expanded into a full-scale production facility in the former Evergreen Nursery building on Groesbeck Highway in Clinton Township. The thirty-five-thousand-square-foot building houses production, cellaring, packaging, distilling, bottling and canning lines; storage; a 250-person tasting room; and administrative offices. The brewhouse contains a 38-barrel brew system with multiple 100- and 120-barrel fermenters that could give it a 26,000-barrel annual capacity. It has extra-high ceilings and added extra warehouse space for further expansion that could provide three to six additional 400-barrel fermenters and the potential to brew up to 75,000 barrels annually. All of this increase in capacity helps get more of the company's beer and mead onto store shelves. The original Warren location brewhouse, taproom and home brew shop remains open. The Kuhnhenn Brewing Company location in Warren shifted its focus to small-batch, barrel-aging and experimental beers and meads.

Kuhnhenn Brewing Company is truly a family-oriented business. The staff is dedicated to making sure that the craft beer consumer has an amazing experience when visiting the taproom or home brew shop. Kuhnhenn hosts

Kuhnhenn Brewing taproom in Warren. *Photo by Erik Smith.*

four major events at the brewery each year. The St. Patrick's Day celebration, Summer Solstice, Oktoberfest and Winter Solstice were created to give back to the very community that has supported it since the company opened in 1998. Each event helps celebrate the changing of the season and the release of many special beers and meads. Since Kuhnhenn Brewing Company has limited space for bottling, it has a special bottle release at each of these events. It is the only time of the year that people can get bottled releases at the brewery. People start lining up early in the morning to get a chance to buy some of these rare and barrel-aged offerings at each of these special events. This dedication to its customers and community is why Kuhnhenn Brewing Company will continue to grow and prosper in the coming years.

FALLING DOWN BEER COMPANY
(2270 EAST 10 MILE ROAD, WARREN)

Mark Larson and George Lang started Falling Down Beer Company in the spring of 2013. They renovated the diner called My Mother's Place in Warren. Although it was an unlikely place to open a brewery, the duo has

Falling Down Beer Company in Warren. *Photo by Erik Smith.*

managed to make it work. Averaging about five hundred barrels per year, the company is gaining a nice following in the area.

Falling Down Beer Company has eight beers on draft at any given time. Standard beers include Ninja Chicken Pale Ale, Rye My Donkey Rye Saison, Angry Beaver Double Brown Ale, Suburban Home IPA, Mother Cluster Cream Ale and Scurvy Dan Blood Orange IPA. New beers are constantly being rotating onto the tap list, and a nice menu of food has plenty of folks taking notice.

Falling Down Beer Company has announced the expansion of operations to a second microbrewery location. The new 4,800-square-foot brewery is located at 14 North Washington Street in Downtown Oxford. It will feature a sixty-seat taproom with thirty taps. Falling Down Beer Company has applied for small wine maker and small distiller licenses for the Oxford location, and the new location is expected to produce two thousand barrels of beer per year or about four times more than the Warren location.

The Warren location will remain open and will also be expanded. Plans are to increase the brewing capacity and obtain a winery license as part of the project. Future plans also include the canning of Falling Down Beer Company's flagship beers Ninja Chicken Pale Ale and Scurvy Dan Blood

Orange IPA. Falling Down Beer Company already distributes beer in the local markets, and with all of the increased brewing capacity, its products should be even more visible on store shelves.

GREAT BARABOO BREWING COMPANY
(35905 UTICA ROAD, CLINTON TOWNSHIP)

Great Baraboo Brewing Company was established in 1995 in what previously housed the Moravian Lodge. It was one of the first brewpubs to open in Michigan once the brewpub law changed in the 1990s and is considered Macomb County's first brewpub.

Great Baraboo Brewing Company is a good-sized brewpub, with a large U-shaped bar and plenty of television screens suitable for watching sports. It also has a regular restaurant seating area and offers a large lunch and dinner menu. The seven-barrel brewhouse is located behind the bar. The standard beers are a wheat ale, golden ale, red ale, porter and brown ale. Additionally, it rotates two to three seasonal selections and one-off beers, as well as offers a few guest taps and a full bar. On any given night, the brewpub has good food and drink specials, as well as activities for its patrons, including Customer Appreciation Night, trivia games, karaoke and live music. The current head brewer, Jeremy Altier, took over in 2012 and has worked hard to brew clean and consistent beers.

To some, Great Baraboo Brewing Company may feel a bit more like a sports bar and restaurant than a brewpub. However, it has been in business for more than twenty years and is still providing good beer and service to the neighborhood.

BAFFIN BREWING COMPANY
(25113 JEFFERSON AVENUE, ST. CLAIR SHORES)

Baffin Brewing Company is located along the Nautical Mile (along Jefferson Avenue between Nine and Ten Mile Roads) of St. Clair Shores. Evan Feringa, Joe Dowd and Joe Vander Marliere started the brewing company in January 2015. It is part of the more recent group of breweries opening in underserved areas of Metro Detroit.

Evan Feringa, co-owner of Baffin Brewing Company in St. Clair Shores. *Photo by Erik Smith.*

The building has housed many different businesses over the years and is one of the oldest buildings in St. Clair Shores. The taproom walls were made with reclaimed brick, and the bar was built with reclaimed lumber. Baffin Brewing Company's name and logo comes from a Bernese mountain dog. The owners' love of four-legged friends can be seen in all of the merchandise that is available for purchase in the taproom.

According to Baffin Brewing Company's website, it "began from a love of craft beer and the community in which the movement was inspired. Our Mission is to provide our customers and community with the very best craft brewery in which to call their own; inspiring a sense of pride with each taste from the glass." Baffin Brewing Company's slogan is, "Follow your Passion. Chase your Tail." The St. Clair Shores community has embraced Baffin Brewing Company, and it serves beer to near capacity crowds on the weekends. It currently does not offer food service, but food can be delivered or brought in from many of the local restaurants in the area. The Baffin Brewing Company also has a unique mug club. To become a member, one needs to consume 150 beers within a year. At each 25-beer increment, a potential member gets a reward (e.g., Baffin Brewing Company sticker, pint glass, T-shirt, growler). Membership is awarded after the 150th beer. Consult the company's website for a listing of the names of its current selections along with a description of each beer. It will be exciting to see how it continues to evolve in the coming years.

ROYAL OAK BREWERY (215 EAST FOURTH STREET, ROYAL OAK)

Drew Ciora founded Royal Oak Brewery in September 1995. It was the first of three brewpubs tied to the aforementioned Beercos, the company Drew started with fellow business partner Mike Plesz. Drew started in the beer industry while living in Huntington Beach, California, where he worked at the Huntington Beach Beer Company. When Mike came to visit Drew, he saw the brewpub model firsthand, and when Drew eventually moved back to Michigan, the rest is history.

ROB, as the locals call it, is considered the oldest operating brewpub in Oakland County. It brews on a fifteen-barrel system and has the capacity to produce one thousand barrels per year. The brewery is located one block east of Main Street and is a very popular place with the locals. ROB currently has more than five hundred mug members.

Royal Oak Brewery offers a comfortable atmosphere and hometown feel. The brewery typically carries eight beers on tap and a few guest taps. The brewery's design is typical of brewpubs from the 1990s, with the serving tanks located directly behind the bar. Guests love seeing where the beer originates, but that can be challenging for the brewers. Space can be rather tight in the bar area at peak times during weeknights and weekends.

No brewery can stay in business unless it consistently brews a solid lineup of beer, and ROB has been making great beer for more than twenty years. Some of the standard beers include Northern Light golden ale, Fourth Street wheat ale, Royal Oak red ale and Royal Pride IPA. Typically, there are two to three seasonal beers to round out the taps.

Man likes to think he can live on beer alone, but a man's also got to eat. Royal Oak Brewery offers a great variety of American comfort food, including mac-and-cheese, burgers, pizza and wings. It also offers a wide range of other food options including Louisiana jambalaya, Korean tacos, Baja fish tacos, Voodoo Curry and shepherd's pie. Royal Oak Brewery offers a free birthday club to all of its guests. Once you sign up, you receive a free

Royal Oak Brewery beer samples. *Photo by Erik Smith.*

entrée and a pint glass on your birthday every year. ROB offers a full bar for those so inclined to imbibe something that isn't beer. During the summer months, it offers a biergarten patio that has been voted "Best Patio" in Metro Detroit numerous times. The brewery provides a haven from the hustle and bustle of Main Street in Royal Oak.

Besides offering mug club members an amazing party each year, Royal Oak Brewery offers plenty of special events. In the summer, it hosts a summer concert series featuring great local artists performing on the brewery's patio. Each September, it also throws an amazing anniversary party. In 2015, ROB celebrated its twentieth anniversary in style with a double-sized party tent, bands, beer and food, and even the mayor of Royal Oak joined the fun. Each month, the brewery offers what it calls a "panel." According to its Facebook post each month, "It's a communal celebration of beer, ROB style. A time to slow your roll and taste the fruit of the malt and the hops. Beer will be spilled and the fat will be chewed. Debate will arise. Opinions will be formed and heard. Fellowship will be had. Nothing will be decided." For ten dollars, customers enjoy a lot of great beer and talk shop with the brewer and brewery regulars alike.

Royal Oak Brewery is a textbook example of a great local brewpub. It continues to serve consistently great beer and food to the Royal Oak community, just like it did when it started more than twenty years ago.

BASTONE BREWERY (419 SOUTH MAIN STREET, ROYAL OAK)

Bastone Brewery opened its doors in the spring of 2004. The brewery's name comes from the famous Belgian city of Bastogne but with a simplified spelling. The brewpub is housed in a 1930s building, the exterior of which has been restored to its original Art Deco look in association with the State Historic Preservation Office. Inside, the high-arched ceiling, wood floors and white subway wall tiles create the comfortable yet sophisticated atmosphere of a European brasserie.

The food menu starts with Belgian-style favorites including steamed mussels and pomme frites and then expands to a variety of items including unique sandwiches, thin-crust pizzas, seafood and salads. The brewery focuses on using the freshest ingredients in its 100 percent from-scratch kitchen.

Standard beers at Bastone include a blonde, pilsner, wit, IPA, dubbel and triple. It typically has a few seasonal beers on tap as well as a full bar with wine and spirits.

One aspect that makes Bastone Brewery unique is that it shares the building with three other bar properties, each with a different concept and all owned by Two Mission Design and Development, the parent company of Bastone Brewery. Vinotecca is a wine bar next door to Bastone that features small plates, cheese samplers, entrées, pizzas and desserts. Monk Beer Abbey is behind Bastone and offers a warm and simply decorated restaurant that pays tribute to the brewing history of Belgium's monasteries and the monks who invented the historic styles. Craft is a cocktail-themed dance club in the basement of Bastone Brewery. Bastone's beers are available in all of the adjoining establishments. Bastone Brewery uses the saying, "One Corner. One Roof." There is not another brewery in Metro Detroit that utilizes space in this way.

The head brewer at Bastone Brewery is Rockne Van Meter. He joined Bastone in 2005, having previously brewed at the former Big Buck Brewery in Auburn Hills and also at Rochester Mills Beer Company in downtown Rochester. Rockne is considered the most award-winning brewer in Michigan. He brews a very consistent lineup of beers for the brewery and for the beer competition circuit.

Beer samples from Bastone Brewery in Royal Oak. *Photo by Erik Smith.*

In 2014, Bastone Brewery and its brew master, Rockne Van Meter, were named Small Brewpub and Small Brewpub Brewer of the Year at the Great American Beer Festival (GABF) in Colorado. The award presented to Bastone was in the category for a brewery that produced fewer than 750 barrels in 2013. More than 1,300 breweries enter beers in the Great American Beer Festival competition among the various categories. It is a very prestigious award to be granted to Bastone. Of all of the great beer awards that Bastone Brewery and its brewer have received over the years, they are very appreciative of this particular honor. According to the GABF website, "The Great American Beer Festival is the premier U.S. beer festival and competition. Each year, GABF represents the largest collection of U.S. beer ever served either in a public tasting event or a private competition. GABF brings together the brewers and diverse beers that place the United States among the world's top brewing nations. GABF was founded in 1982, and it has been growing and evolving along with the American craft brewing industry ever since." The Great American Beer Festival is the largest beer competition and festival in North America, drawing more than sixty thousand visitors to it each year. It is the one beer competition that all brewers strive to be part of and where brewers aspire to win awards.

Lily's Seafood Grill and Brewery
(410 South Washington Street, Royal Oak)

Bob and Scott Morton run Lily's Seafood Grill and Brewery. They started out running a few restaurants and brewpubs in Florida. The brothers eventually sold their two Florida brewpubs, Ragtime Tavern and A1A Ales Works, in 1996 to Craftworks Restaurants & Brewery Inc. Craftworks is the parent company of Rock Bottom Brewery, Gordon Biersch and Old Chicago chains. Both of the brewpubs they sold are still in business today.

After the sale of the Florida brewpubs, Bob Morton moved back to Michigan and starting selling brewery equipment for DME Brewing Solutions. DME Brewing Solutions is a leader in the craft beer brewing industry with more than twenty-two years of experience and has become the preferred supplier of equipment to craft brewing customers around the world. Scott Morton eventually followed his brother and moved back to Michigan in 1997. Both men returned to Michigan because of their roots in the Detroit area. The brothers grew up in Redford and still have family in that area today.

At first, the city of Royal Oak was hesitant at the idea of having breweries within its city limits. The city thought that breweries could turn the downtown area into a party district. However, instead of just opening up a brewery, Bob and Scott replicated their successful Florida business model of a seafood restaurant and brewpub. In 1999, the brothers opened Lily's Seafood Grill and Brewery on Washington Street in Royal Oak. They named the restaurant and brewpub after their grandmother Lily A. Strange, a Scottish immigrant. Customers can easily see their grandmother's influence all over Lily's, from the homemade food to the hand-crafted beer to the childhood family photos that are displayed throughout the brewpub. Lily's Seafood Grill & Brewery is truly a family operation.

Lily's is housed in a former 1930s S.S. Kresge store. The building eventually housed an office supply store and fitness center before Bob and Scott Morton completely gutted the interior to make way for their restaurant and brewpub. The restaurant and brewpub's décor provides a relaxed setting split between the main restaurant seating area and the bar seating in the front. During the warmer months, Lily's offers one of the best outdoor seating areas in Royal Oak. The restaurant displays local artwork on a rotating basis, typically featuring six to eight artists a year. The artwork adds to the homey feel of the restaurant and brewery.

Scott Morton is the brew master at Lily's, with help from his son, Marlon. They brew on a five-barrel system with an average output of six hundred barrels per year. With Scott's thirty-plus years of brewing experience, he is teaching Marlon the finer points of brewing on a smaller brew system. As Scott put it, "We brew micro-biologically sound beer for our customers." As customers have become better educated about beer styles and their tastes have diversified, so, too, have the beers that Lily's offers. Scott and Marlon offer a wide range of beer styles. To please any palate, they offer a high-quality lineup of beers spanning many styles from wheat, wit and hefeweizen to pilsner, pale ale and IPA to amber, porter and stout. In 2015, Lily's recently upgraded its draft system from an eight-tap to a twelve-tap tower.

Once a month, Lily's treats its beer mug club members right with two-dollar pint nights. It offers a similar monthly special for its wine club. Lily's also offers a lifetime mug club membership for fifty dollars, which gives members a T-shirt, discounts on pints and growlers and their initial growler fill for free. Annually, Lily's offers a beer bus tour and wine bus tour to various breweries and wineries in the state of Michigan and beyond. Every April,

Interior of Lily's Seafood & Brewery in Royal Oak. *Photo by Stephen Johnson.*

Lily's Seafood & Brewery in Royal Oak. *Photo by Stephen Johnson.*

Lily's hosts Tartan Day to pay homage to the family's roots. Tartan Day is a celebration of their Scottish heritage, and Lily's pulls out all of the stops with a truly authentic Scottish menu. It orders the haggis from Ackroyds Scottish bakery in Redford, the same bakery that the brothers visited as kids.

Lily's offers great happy hour specials from 2:00 p.m. to 6:00 p.m. Monday through Friday and a build-your-own Bloody Mary bar on the weekends. There are plenty of annual themed events that have gained a very loyal following over the years. Lily's is open 364 days a year and offers special buffet menus for Mother's Day, Easter and Thanksgiving. At Lily's, the food is no afterthought. The staff cuts all of the potatoes and makes all of the sauces, soups and amazing desserts. The food is all handmade on site to accompany each of the freshly brewed beers. The consistent attention to detail and focus on quality products and service is why Lily's has been a staple in the Royal Oak restaurant and beer scene for more than fifteen years.

RIVER ROUGE BREWING COMPANY
(406 EAST FOURTH STREET, ROYAL OAK)

River Rouge Brewing Company opened in May 2015 in the former Knights of Columbus building on Fourth Street just one block east of longtime brewpub Royal Oak Brewery. Brothers Edward and Chip Stencel with help from Chip's wife, Martha, operate the brewery. River Rouge Brewing Company gets its name from the Michigan city where the Stencels' grandfather grew up.

Edward Stencel was previously in the film industry and traveled the world as a cinematographer and producer. He studied brewing under Alex Van Horne, owner and head brewer of San Diego's Intergalactic Brewing Company. Edward wears a work shirt with the River Rouge Brewing Company logo embroidered on one side and the Intergalactic Brewing Company logo on the opposite, thereby paying homage to his West Coast brewery comrades.

River Rouge Brewing Company is considered a nanobrewery and brews on a three-barrel system. (Although there is no official definition of a nanobrewery, many feel it is one that brews three barrels or less, and it usually does not brew more than one batch at a time.) River Rouge Brewing Company has a small tasting room that can accommodate thirty people. It

Left: Stroh's Bohemian Style Beer label. *Photo by Noreen Johnson.*

Below: Pfeiffer Famous Beer label. *Photo by Noreen Johnson.*

Above: Bock Beer label. *Photo by Noreen Johnson.*

Left: Stroh's Bohemian Style Beer bottle. *Photo by Noreen Johnson.*

Above: Stroh's beer tap handles. *Photo by Noreen Johnson.*

Right: Altes Golden Lager Beer can. *Photo by Noreen Johnson.*

Above: Double Bock Beer label. *Photo by Noreen Johnson.*

Left: Goebel Beer bottle. *Photo by Noreen Johnson.*

Above: Stroh's Brewery beer truck. *Photo by Noreen Johnson.*

Right: Antique beer bottle capper. *Photo by Noreen Johnson.*

Stroh's beer bottle caps. *Photo by Noreen Johnson.*

E&B Brewery site tile mosaic. *Photo by Stephen Johnson.*

Motor City Brewing Works & Winery fermenters. *Photo by Stephen Johnson.*

Motor City Brewing Works & Winery front sign. *Photo by Stephen Johnson.*

Stroh's Brewery manual cover. *From* Stroh's: The Fire Brewing Story.

Stroh's Brewery beer lineup. *From* Stroh's: The Fire Brewing Story.

Old Atwater Block Brewery sign. *Photo by Stephen Johnson.*

Atwater Brewery brewhouse. *Photo by Stephen Johnson.*

Ascension Brewery Company brewhouse. *Photo by Erik Smith.*

Kevin DeGrood of North Center Brewing Company posing in the brewhouse. *Photo by Erik Smith.*

Batch Brewing in Detroit beer glasses. *Photo by Erik Smith.*

Beer sample tray. *Photo by Erik Smith.*

Above: Fenton Winery & Brewery beer glass. *Photo by Erik Smith.*

Left: Atwater in the Park taproom in Grosse Pointe Park. *Photo by Stephen Johnson.*

River Edge Brewing Company in Milford. *Photo by Erik Smith.*

Beer
sampler
from
River
Edge
Brewing
Company
in
Milford.
*Photo by
Erik Smith.*

Brewery tanks at Griffin Claw Brewing Company in Birmingham. *Photo by Erik Smith*.

Royal Oak Brewery beer samples. *Photo by Erik Smith*.

Tap handles from Dragonmead Brewery in Warren. *Photo by Noreen Johnson.*

Bock Beer. *Courtesy of Library of Congress.*

Left: John Linardos of Motor City Brewing Works in Detroit giving a brewery tour. *Photo by Noreen Johnson.*

Below: JT of CJ's Brewing Company in Commerce Township brewing on the pilot system. *Photo by Noreen Johnson.*

Beer samples. *Photo by Erik Smith.*

keeps limited hours, so customers should check out the brewery's website prior to visiting. The beer list is constantly changing but has a focus on British-style ales with a bit higher alcohol content. Some typical beers on draft include brown ale, stout, vanilla porter, coffee blonde ale, mango ale, honey golden ale, pale ale and IPA. River Rouge Brewing Company is just down the road from Royal Oak Brewery and across the street from Motor City Gas, a whiskey distillery. The nearness of the three businesses to one another makes the area a nice stop for any craft beer enthusiast.

ROAK BREWING (330 EAST LINCOLN AVENUE, ROYAL OAK)

Roak Brewing became the newest kid on the block in Royal Oak when its doors opened in June 2015. The Roak founders are John Leone, Chuck Mascari and Chuck Mascari Jr., who together bring many years of food and beverage experience to the world of craft beer. They hired head brewer Brandon MacClaren and an experienced brew team to get Roak off the

Roak Brewing in Royal Oak. *Photo by Stephen Johnson.*

ground. Brandon has previously worked on the west side of the state at New Holland Brewery in Holland and Founders Brewing in Grand Rapids.

The taproom is an impressive sight, decorated with a very modern look and feel. The taproom, modest in size, has seating for seventy people inside and twenty-eight outside and offers a limited food menu of pizza, salads and panini. The name Roak comes from a combination of the words *royal* and *oak*. In Europe, "roak" means smoke—where there is smoke there is fire. As patrons enter the taproom, they see two large fiery banners on either side of the U-shaped bar, with each having a Doberman pinscher graphic toward the banner's bottom edge. A large beautiful jeweled chandelier hangs in the center of the taproom, and the entire right side of the taproom has windows for customers to get a glimpse into the production brewery.

Don't let the taproom's size fool you into thinking it's a small operation. The production brewery is sixteen thousand square feet in size. The brewhouse contains a 30-barrel main brew system and a 10-barrel pilot system. Roak has already purchased additional fermenters to keep up with market demand. It currently has the capacity to brew 13,500 barrels annually, giving it plenty of room to grow. Roak distributes its beers on draft and bottles in southeast Michigan. It has six core beers that include Live IPA, Powerboat Belgian

White, Devil Dog Oatmeal Stout, Around the Clock Session IPA, Mean Street ESB and Kashmir Belgian Dark Strong Ale. Roak Brewing also has sixteen beers on draft at any time in the taproom and seems to be always experimenting with new beer recipes.

WOODWARD AVENUE BREWERS (22646 WOODWARD AVENUE, FERNDALE)

Chris and Krista Johnston and Chris's brother, Grant, opened Woodward Avenue Brewers in 1997. They were part of the first wave of brewpubs to hit Oakland County. The brewery is located on Woodward Avenue, just south of Nine Mile Road, right in the heart of Ferndale. Woodward Avenue Brewers was an important anchor to the eventual development that has occurred in Ferndale over the last fifteen years. It has a very eclectic Detroit-focused décor that customers enjoy.

Beer samples from Woodward Avenue Brewers in Ferndale. *Photo by Erik Smith.*

The owners of Woodward Avenue Brewers also operate two sister properties on either side of the brewery. The Emory Restaurant across the street opened in 2006 and offers a diverse menu of burgers, sandwiches, pasta and salads. The Loving Touch pool hall next door to the brewery opened in 2008. It offers a great place to play pool and check out local music. The three properties give the owners plenty of projects to keep them busy in this bustling section of Ferndale. According to the website, "Woodward Avenue Brewers has been putting the ALE in FerndALE since 1997."

Current head brewer Greg Burke has been with Woodward Avenue Brewers for many years and has crafted a very consistent lineup of quality beers. The standard ones include blonde ale, raspberry blonde ale, hefeweizen, vanilla porter, steam beer and a couple of solid IPAs. Greg also constantly rotates seasonal beers into the lineup, and he offers samplers, half and full pints, as well as growlers-to-go. In addition to beer, Woodward Avenue Brewers offers a full bar with hard cider, wine and spirits.

Woodward Avenue Brewers offers the Ferndale community many reasons to keep coming back. It offers two-dollar pints on Sunday and great happy hour specials during the week. The menu was recently revamped to include pizzas, calzones, salads and sandwiches. With first-floor seating that includes open patio views of Woodward and a solid lineup of beers, Woodward Avenue Brewers is a great local brewpub of which the Ferndale community can be proud.

Black Lotus Brewing Company
(1 East 14 Mile Road, Clawson)

Mark Harper, Michael Allan and Jodi Allan (Mark's sister) founded Black Lotus Brewing Company. Mark was a school psychologist, and Mike was a financial planner. Both men had grown disenchanted of the daily grind and longed to chart a new course in life. They took that leap by opening Black Lotus Brewing Company in downtown Clawson in 2006.

The founders have created the business philosophy "Think Global, Drink Local." Under this philosophy, Black Lotus has committed itself to creating quality beer and food for the Clawson community. People entering the Black Lotus Brewing Company cannot help but feel a relaxed coffeehouse kind of vibe. The brewery is decorated in darker tones with a great lounge area for relaxation. While it does have the typical table and bar setting, as patrons spend more time there, they recognize the more laid-back, comfortable style of the brewpub.

Nicholas Joseph was brought onto the brew staff in 2015. Nick brings with him prior brewery experience that will help Mark Harper keep a consistent beer lineup on tap at the brewery. They have already taken advantage of the extra staff by adding barrel aging into their arsenal. The standard beers include cream ale, wheat ale, amber ale, oatmeal stout, pale ale, ESB and an IPA. Black Lotus also has some great seasonal offerings that include a summer saison and a barley wine. In addition to house beers, they have guest taps, local and national spirits, mead, wine and hard cider. Great happy hour specials are offered Monday to Friday from 4:00 p.m. to 6:00 p.m., with half-off house beers along with food specials. Black Lotus Brewing Company offers a food menu that features burgers, salads and sandwiches. When the weather turns cold, be sure to try the turkey chili.

Great beer and food is only half of the story at Black Lotus Brewing Company. Besides being one of the brewery's founders, Mark Harper is also an accomplished musician. His band, Zap Toro, plays at Black Lotus Brewing Company every Tuesday. Zap Toro is a world groove, Detroit-based project of Mark's. The group specializes in a wide array of music styles that spans the globe. Additionally, Black Lotus Brewing Company hosts an open mic night every Monday. Whether you like hip-hop, jazz, world music or anything in between, Black Lotus offers lots of great entertainment options to keep you grooving to your own beat.

Next door to Black Lotus Brewing Company is the Drive In. It started out as a golf-simulator entertainment space. The owners of Black Lotus purchased the space adjacent to the brewery and opened up the wall between the two spaces. By doing so, it offers patrons a chance to rent golf time by the hour while still enjoying Black Lotus beer and food. It has been a popular rental space for corporate groups and social outings since it opened. In 2015, it was remodeled to create a more intimate space for live music.

Whether you come to Black Lotus Brewing Company to enjoy a good beer, good eats or good tunes or you have a good golf swing, you are assured to have a good time. The city of Clawson is lucky to have such a great brewery anchor in its town.

GRIFFIN CLAW BREWING COMPANY
(575 SOUTH ETON STREET, BIRMINGHAM)

Griffin Claw Brewing Company, which opened its doors in July 2013, is owned by Bonnie LePage and Mary Nicholson. Norm LePage (Bonnie's husband) and Ray Nicholson (Mary's husband) are the co-owners of the nearby Big Rock Chophouse and the Reserve banquet facility. Griffin Claw Brewing Company initially invested $5 million to build the brewhouse, taproom, biergarten and distribution facility. The property where the brewery was built was originally slated to be condominiums, but the opportunity for the location was too great to pass up with the craft beer movement kicking into high gear. The duo built a twelve-thousand-square-foot, state-of-the-art facility that would make any craft beer enthusiast's mouth water. The taproom seats one hundred people, and during the summer months, the taproom opens up to allow seventy-five people to sit outside in the communal seating of the authentic biergarten. The taproom offers casual food items that accompany the amazing beer list, and both are sure to satisfy any appetite.

Having a fancy state-of-the-art brewery is one part of the puzzle, but great beer is needed to win over craft beer consumers. Griffin Claw Brewing Company has that covered. Its master brewer is Dan Rogers, who got his professional start as a chef in Las Vegas. In 1992, Dan helped open Big Dog's Brewing Company, the first brewery in Las Vegas. In 1999, he made his way back to his home state of Michigan, where he worked at the now defunct Michigan Brewing Company in Webberville. Big Rock Chophouse brought him on board as its head brewer in 2004. At Big Rock Chophouse, Dan built up an amazing list of brewing awards for his beer. He has won nine gold medals, six silver and four bronze awards from various national and international beer competitions, including a gold medal for the best IPA in the world in 2010 for what is now Griffin Claw's flagship beer, Norm's Raggedy Ass IPA. The owners of Big Rock decided to take their award-winning brewer and the entire brewhouse out of Big Rock to create the Griffin Claw Brewing Company complex. Dan Rogers is the head brewer, distiller and director of brewing operations at Griffin Claw.

Griffin Claw Brewing Company's standard beers include Norm's Raggedy Ass IPA, Grand Trunk Bohemian Pilsner, El Rojo Red Ale, Grind Line Pale Ale, Platinum Blonde Ale, Norm's Gateway IPA and Mr. Blue Sky. It also offers many seasonal and specialty beers, most of which are only available at the taproom and to-go in special twenty-three-ounce bottles and growlers. It sells its standard beers and select seasonal ones in cans and on draft throughout Michigan.

In addition to producing award-winning beers, Griffin Claw produces spirits. Two ninety-gallon German pot stills were installed and are used to produce vodka and gin. The spirits are currently sold by the glass in the brewery's taproom, but they will eventually be available in bottles at select retail locations.

Griffin Claw Brewing Company will be an exciting brewery to watch in the coming years. It has a unique combination of brewery talent and business experience that should help it continue to grow throughout the state of Michigan and beyond.

AXLE BREWING COMPANY (4847 DELEMERE AVENUE, ROYAL OAK)

Scott King is considered one of the early Michigan craft beer pioneers and original members of the Michigan Brewers Guild. He started out in the brewing industry in 1994, when he opened King Brewing Company. He located his microbrewery northwest of downtown Pontiac in an industrial area. It was the first microbrewery in Oakland County since Prohibition ended. King worked hard and gained a good following in the local market. However, a bad real estate deal forced Scott King to close the doors of the brewpub for good in 2009 after fifteen years of business. Sometimes when one door closes, a new door opens, and it was not long until Scott was up and running with his next brewing venture.

Scott and his business partner Kristy Smith founded MillKing It Productions (MIP) in 2010. They had a simple approach to brewing beer. They wanted to "strip down all pretensions and preconceived notions of the craft brewing industry and create a truly memorable and focused catalog of fine beers." MIP beer, as it was known in the marketplace, worked out of an unobtrusive industrial building in Royal Oak. MIP beers were one of the first craft beers within Michigan to be canned. Canning versus bottling offers a superior way to preserve beer, as canning beer protects it from harmful light that can degrade the quality and flavor of the beer. Cans are also lighter to ship and better for the environment. With that in mind, MIP beer was only available in cans and on draft. MillKing It Productions produced a stable lineup of beers that included AXL Pale Ale, BRIK Irish Red Ale, SNO Belgian White Ale and some great seasonal beers.

Axle Brewing Company was the next phase in the life of Scott King and his brewing team. Formed in the fall of 2015, Axle Brewing Company is the housed in the same building as the former MIP beer. With new investors, new branding and new beers, Scott King has a new lease on life. In September 2015, Axle Brewing Company's beers hit the marketplace in cans and on draft in the Metro Detroit area. The standard beers include WIT Belgian White Ale, red ale, porter, IPA, Frank Black IPA and Ruby Red IPA. With all of the experience that Scott King has had in the craft beer industry, continued success is the forecast for Axle Brewing Company.

Sherwood Brewing Company
(45689 Hayes Road, Shelby Township)

Sherwood Brewing Company opened its doors in August 2006. It offers handcrafted beer, wine, mead, hard cider and sodas, all made on site. Sherwood Brewing was part of the second wave of craft breweries that opened in the Detroit area. To provide a reference point as to the growth of Michigan's craft beer industry, in 2006 Sherwood Brewing was the seventy-second license issued. By the end of 2015, Michigan numbered in the two hundreds for brewery licenses issued.

Ray and Lisa Sherwood founded Sherwood Brewing Company. Ray and brewer/manager Corey Paul handle the brewing duties, with Lisa handling the management side of the business. Sherwood uses the slogan "Making obnoxiously unpretentious beers." As Ray Sherwood explained it in a Mittenbrew.com website article, "We're almost obnoxious about not being pretentious." Sherwood brews great approachable beers that are sure to please the palate.

Ray Sherwood started out home brewing in the 1990s while he was in college. After college, he returned to Detroit and started brewing at Kuhnhenn Brewing in Warren. Kuhnhenn is a family brewery business run by Eric Jr. and Brett Kuhnhenn and their father, Eric Sr. At Kuhnhenn, Ray learned a lot about running a brewery from the ground up. It has been said that it can take a village to run a brewery. Working for family-run Kuhnhenn Brewing Company allowed Ray to see how everyone in the family chips in to make the operation work. When he left Kuhnhenn Brewing Company, Ray had a vision of what he wanted for his own brewery.

Beer samples from Sherwood Brewing Company in Shelby Township. *Photo by Erik Smith.*

Sherwood Brewing Company brews on a seven-barrel brew system. It purchased the brew system from a brewery that had closed. Ray and Corey have been able to use the small but versatile system to brew a wide range of beers, meads and ciders since they opened in 2006. Sherwood Brewing produced seven hundred barrels of beer in 2015. Eleven beers are kept on draft, including Alaskan Sister Wit, Buxom BlonDDe Ale and Mistress Jade's Hemp Ale. The brewery also has plenty of rotating seasonal beers including Cork County Red Ale, Disco Lemonade and Smoked Pumpkin Porter. Besides beer, Sherwood Brewing offers multiple meads, wines and sodas to quench a thirst.

When someone thinks of visiting a brewery, the local strip mall does not immediately come to mind. However, Sherwood has been able to create a very relaxed and open atmosphere in the middle of a strip mall–centric area of Shelby Township. Visitors can see the brewing process and smell the beer immediately upon entering. It is not hidden away. Ray and Corey like to have customers see where and how the beer gets produced. The brewers also like to keep an open dialogue between their customers and themselves.

Just three days prior to their 2006 opening, Sherwood Brewing hired Corey Paul. Corey credited his grandma for finding the want ad for a prep cook at Sherwood Brewing. Previously, he had worked in the restaurant industry and had also been home brewing. Ray and Lisa needed someone who could run a kitchen. It was a unique match. Today, Corey still oversees the kitchen, but he also splits the brewing duties and recipe development with Ray. This arrangement allows them both to learn from each other and develop their crafts.

The décor of the brewery has grown to include a respectable variety of beer collectibles. Sherwood has growlers and bottles from other breweries displayed around the brewery walls, as well as old beer signs and a retro beer fridge. Some of the beer décor came from the owners' personal collection, and customers have brought in other pieces. It has really come together over time and gives the brewery a comfortable and homey feel.

Sherwood Brewing Company offers what it calls a "mugless club" for its customers, which is a mug club without the numbered mug that most breweries offer. Instead of storing a large number of mugs, Sherwood Brewing Company serves its mugless club members a beer in a twenty-ounce glass. The mugless club offers plenty of discounts, quarterly appreciation parties and special releases to its nearly one thousand active members. Every Monday, Sherwood offers mugless Mondays. Members can bring in any mug and fill it to a maximum of thirty ounces at regular pint prices. Members also get half-off appetizers and two dollars off growler fills. Sherwood offers specials for the rest of its customers as well. Monday through Saturday, Sherwood has the best daily lunch specials in town and two dollars off beers from 11:30 a.m. to 3:00 p.m. Monday through Friday, Sherwood offers "hoppy hour" from 3:00 p.m. to 6:00 p.m. with one dollar off beer and wine.

Sherwood Brewing also offers plenty of entertainment for its customers, including Quizzo trivia on Tuesdays, blues music on Wednesdays and live music on most Saturdays. Twice a year, Sherwood runs a fun brewery event called Beer Factor. It is Sherwood Brewery's version of *Fear Factor*. Contestants answer trivia and perform eating and strength challenges. The winner gets his/her first beer on the house each time he/she comes into the brewery for up to six months.

Sherwood Brewing Company is a family-friendly brewery. During peak dinner hours, entire families come in to eat and drink. The parents can enjoy beer and wine, and the kids can enjoy a freshly made soda. The brewery offers a full food menu of appetizers, sandwiches, burgers, pizza and desserts. (Ask for the beer or wine sauce pizza when you visit.) Over the last few years, Sherwood Brewing has made an effort to make more of its food from scratch. The brewery has always tried to source food locally, and a few years ago, the brewery even went microwave free. In the winter of 2015, Sherwood Brewing rolled out a new food menu with all the items now prepared in-house. It is just one of the many ways Sherwood Brewing has worked to distance itself from the average bar or restaurant and provide healthier ingredients for its food.

Sherwood Brewing offers special beer pairing dinners throughout the year. Beer and cheese, beer and wild game and beer and chocolate have been some of the past beer pairings. It has always worked on new and innovative ways to increase the customer's enjoyment of its products. On select shopping related holidays, Sherwood offers the "man cave" wherein the brewery becomes a hidden sanctuary from the shopping malls of Macomb County. Men can come and enjoy a kegs-and-eggs breakfast while watching some sports in the friendly confines of the brewery. Sherwood Brewing offers its customers many other special events each year. In September, it has "Wood Fest," which includes the releases of a small-batch beer, live music and a pig roast. In October, it celebrates Oktoberfest with German-inspired cuisine and the release of the fest beer.

Sherwood Brewing is also a big fan of disc golf. If you have ever sampled Sherwood Brewing's beer at the Michigan Brewers Guild's Summer Beer Festival in Ypsilanti, Michigan, you might have noticed the disc golf cage set up next to where the staff was pouring you that beer. If you threw a disc and it landed in the cage, you won a T-shirt. It draws big crowds each year. Each year, Sherwood Brewing sponsors an annual disc golf tournament at Stoney Creek Metro Park called the Morning Wood Classic. The event has continued to grow in popularity and draws hundreds. Furthermore, Sherwood sponsors other disc golf events around Metro Detroit in conjunction with Discraft out of Wixom.

Sherwood Brewing Company has been the recipient of WDIV's "4 the Best" Award for the Best Brewpub for nine consecutive years, which is proof that the people of Shelby Township (and beyond) love what Sherwood Brewing Company is doing.

Brooks Brewing (52033 Van Dyke, Shelby Township)

Brooks Brewing is the newest kid on the block in Macomb County. It swung open its doors in September 2015. It is housed in a strip mall between 23 Mile and 24 Mile Roads. The brewery is large and spacious at five thousand square feet and includes the brewhouse and taproom. It currently has twelve taps of beer with plans to add on more in the future. The hope is that as the business grows, it will be able to sell bottled and draft products in Macomb County bars, restaurants and retailers.

Like Kuhnhenn Brewery, Brooks Brewing is also a family affair. It was started by Cary Brooks Jr., who is the brewer, with help from his father, Cary Brooks Sr., and brothers, Ken and Rob. According to the Brooks Brewing website, "Brooks Brewing is the result of a love for high quality beer that runs deep within our family. We're a family of born tinkerers, craftsmen, and learners who have a thirst for knowledge and perfection of our respective trades. We pride ourselves on learning the ins-and-outs of everything we do. Our backgrounds are rich in the arts and empirical sciences—assets we apply to our everyday work at Brooks Brewing."

Brooks Brewing is currently focused on making the best beer and wine possible. Although the brewery does not serve food, patrons may bring in their own food or order it delivered. Catering and/or food truck service is usually available on Fridays and Saturdays.

A HISTORY OF BREWING IN THE MOTOR CITY

Granite City Food & Brewery
(699 West Big Beaver Road, Troy /
39603 Traditions Drive, Northville)

Granite City Food & Brewery is a regional chain started in St. Cloud, Minnesota, in 1999. Granite City is the nickname for St. Cloud, one of the great granite capitals of the world.

Granite City Food & Brewery has grown to thirty-five locations in fourteen states. There are now three locations in Michigan, all in the Detroit area. The first location opened in Troy in 2012. This property is positioned in a popular business and retail district of Troy and close to I-75. It has quickly become a popular destination for lunch and dinner business since its opening. In 2015, Granite City Food & Brewery opened its second Michigan location in Northville. It followed the same successful formula used in Troy by locating it in a popular business and retail district of Northville. The third Michigan location will be opening in 2016 in the Renaissance Center in downtown Detroit. The plan is to have a more upscale dining experience with a multi-tap beer bar that features its house beer as well as many other craft beer options.

The brewery uses a patented brewing process called "Fermentus Interruptus." It brews beer at a central brewing facility and ships the liquid wort to each Granite City location to ferment on site. This process allows Granite City to be more efficient and able to replicate the same quality beer throughout all Granite City locations.

Granite City Food & Brewery's signature brews include the Duke Pale Ale, the Bennie Bock, the Batch 1000 Double IPA, the Northern Light Lager and the stout. It offers rotating seasonal brews throughout the year, as well as a full bar and very attractive happy hour prices. It sells its house beers to-go in growlers and also offers a very reasonably priced lifetime mug club membership.

The brewery takes the food part of its name very seriously. It offers an extensive menu of American cuisine, from appetizers, salads, soups, pasta, pizza and sandwiches to steaks, ribs, pork chops and seafood. It offers a free frequent-diner rewards program whereby the customer earns points on all food purchases, and those points can be redeemed toward money off future visits. Granite City Food & Brewery offers catering and private room dining options at all of its locations.

DETROIT BEER

ROCHESTER MILLS BEER COMPANY
(400 WATER STREET, ROCHESTER)

Mike Plesz opened the Rochester Mills Beer Company brewpub in 1998. The brewpub is located in a historic building just two blocks east of downtown Rochester. It was the second of three brewpubs that Mike helped open as a partner in Beercos, the company he and his former business partner Drew Ciora started. Mike also helped open Royal Oak Brewery in 1995 and Detroit Beer Company in 2003. The two partners have now split, but Mike continued with Rochester Mills Beer Company, while Drew kept his stake in Royal Oak Brewery and Detroit Beer Company. In addition to having prior business ventures together, family ties also connect Drew and Mike since Drew married Mike's sister, Michelle. Drew and Mike were always interested in creating brewpubs that were part of the local community, and buildings in all three of their brewpub projects were historic renovations. The building that houses Rochester Mills Beer Company was used as a milling operation for Western Knitting Mill from the 1800s to 1939. The building has served as home to several businesses over the years and was eventually restored in 1998, and Rochester Mills Beer Company has been an anchor tenant since that time.

The Rochester Mills Beer Company brewpub offers beer-to-go in cans, growlers or kegs, and there are plenty of beer and food specials at the brewpub. It offers three-dollar pints on Monday to Friday from 4:00 p.m. to 6:00 p.m., the Tuesday and Thursday specials are six-dollar growler fills and Fridays and Saturdays have free live music. The brewpub's menu features a wide selection of American cuisine to quench whatever hunger patrons may have. The brewpub has pool tables, spacious indoor seating, outdoor patio seating in summer and live entertainment on the weekends. The Lazy Daze Lounge is the private bar space in the back of the brewpub. It regularly hosts private parties and special events, particularly popular for people celebrating life events such as birthdays, anniversaries, wedding showers, retirements and even wakes. Rochester Mills Beer Company continues to earn the distinction of the top beer-producing brewpub in the state of Michigan by producing over more than 1,200 barrels of beer annually from the pub location.

Rochester Mills Beer Company's brewpub typically has fourteen house beers on draft. It produces year-round beers that include Lazy Daze Amber, Milkshake Stout, Rochester Red, Pine Knob Pilsner and Cornerstone IPA. It also offers many pub exclusive beers that include Organic Wit, Water Street Wheat, ESB, porter and pale ale. Additionally, it constantly offers seasonal selections to keep customers returning to the pub.

Rochester Mills offers some great amenities to its customers. It has a free birthday club that allows patrons to get a free entrée on his/her birthday each year. A mug club member gets discounted beer from his/her own numbered twenty-ounce mug, enjoys an annual mug club party and has opportunities to attend beer dinners and special beer releases at discounted rates, all for just thirty-five dollars per year. It also has a bike club for fifty dollars per year for new memberships and forty dollars per year for renewals. With the bike club membership, members get 15 percent off food and drink, an annual club party, discounts at local bike shops and a weekly group bike ride every Tuesday and Thursday. Group rides leave from the rear parking lot of the brewpub, which is located near the downtown Rochester paved walking and bike path. The paved path can connect riders to the Paint Creek or Clinton River rail trails. The bikers ride for two hours and return to the brewpub for food and drinks. On any given night, there may be twenty to thirty riders joining the ride.

Rochester Mills holds many annual events for its customers and the surrounding Rochester community. Every September, it kicks off the fall season with its Oktoberfest celebration. Guests can enjoy German-style cuisine, live music, plenty of beer and a variety of activities for all ages. A unique feature of the festival is the chance to purchase an actual Munich Oktoberfest beer stein during the event. Rochester Mills imports the steins straight from Germany. This festival has grown to be one of the largest Oktoberfest celebrations in the state, and proceeds from the festival benefit local charities.

One of the flagship beer brands at Rochester Mills Beer Company is Milkshake Stout. It is now the brewpub's biggest seller in the local market. At Christmas time, the brewpub celebrates this beer by offering the "12 Days of Milkshake Stout." The base of the sweet stout offers lots of great flavor profiles that can be blended into it. Rochester Mills has created Imperial, bourbon barrel aged and even blueberry pancake versions of the beer for this popular promotion. It offers a special beer release for each of the twelve days at the brewpub and at bars across Michigan. It is a celebration of tasty stout beer just in time for the Christmas holidays.

Rochester Mills Beer Company's head brewer is Eric Briggeman. Like many of the early brewers, Eric had an unconventional path that brought him into the professional brewing world. He was attending Oakland University in the 1990s and was studying human resource management. Eric was not really sure what he wanted to do with his life at that time, and then he saw an ad in the *Michigan Beer Guide* stating that a new location of Big

Buck Brewery was planning to open in Auburn Hills. When Eric vacationed in northern Michigan, he would stop at the Big Buck Brewery in Gaylord. So, Eric mailed his résumé and applied for the job of assistant brewer.

After a few months, Scott Graham, the corporate brewer for Big Buck in Gaylord, contacted Eric and offered him the job of assistant brewer for Big Buck Brewery in Auburn Hills. Eric had done some home brewing, but he had little experience brewing on a big scale. Thus, Scott had Eric come to Big Buck in Gaylord and be trained on its system. In August 1997, Big Buck Brewery in Auburn Hills opened up with Eric at the helm as the main brewer. Bill Wambly and Forrest Knapp eventually joined the team as brewers in Auburn Hills. Big Buck Brewery eventually closed, and Eric, Bill and Forrest now work for Rochester Mills Beer Company. Forrest leads the brewing activities at the brewpub, and Eric and Bill run the show at the production brewery. Eric Briggeman is also the current president of the Michigan Brewers Guild. Eric has been part of the board since 2003 and has served as president since 2007. Scott Graham, Eric's former boss at Big Buck Brewery, is now the executive director of the Michigan Brewers Guild.

Mike Plesz expanded the Rochester Mills Beer Company brand in 2012 when he opened its production brewery in Auburn Hills. It is located in an industrial area just south of the Palace of Auburn Hills. While the brewpub focuses on brewing and sales of beer on the premises, the production brewery focuses on brewing beer for distribution in the marketplace. Rochester Mills Beer Company's distribution partners have worked hard to get their beer in draft form to bars and restaurants and in cans to retailers throughout Michigan. The Rochester Mills production brewery is a forty-six-thousand-square-foot plant that houses a fifty-barrel brewhouse with one-hundred-barrel fermenters. The modern brew system is capable of producing sixty thousand barrels of beer annually. The production brewery has room to grow as the Rochester Mills Beer Company brands develop and grow in the marketplace. The standard beers that are served at the brewpub are all sold in draft and cans out of the production brewery. The company is currently selling its beer throughout Michigan and select parts of Ohio and Florida. Down the road, it hopes to can some of its seasonal beers and expand its barrel aging program. It will be exciting to watch the company develop and grow in the future.

51 North Brewing (51 North Broadway, Lake Orion)

51 North Brewing opened in Lake Orion in January 2013. The brewery is housed in a building that dates back to 1932. The building was a former gas station in the 1930s and a car dealership in the 1950s and 1960s and then was divided up to house multiple businesses in the 1990s. In 2005, the Village of Lake Orion purchased the building and used it for the downtown Development Authority's office. After a few years of working with the city of Lake Orion, Don and Mary Gindhart were able to take over the building, and 51 North Brewing was born. Don was a home brewer for many years and was fortunate to work with some great brewers in the 1990s during the first craft beer wave in Michigan. Don shadowed under Kuhnhenn Brewing Company in early 2000. With its support, Don was able to see firsthand what it takes to run a brewery.

Don is an accomplished musician, playing guitar and bass and singing in various bands over the years. Don heads up the live entertainment at 51 North Brewing Company. The brewery offers an open mic night on Tuesdays, acoustic music on Thursdays, live music on Fridays and Saturdays and jazz on Sundays. It is clear that the owners love all kinds of music and offer something for everyone.

Beer list from 51 North Brewery in Lake Orion. *Photo by Erik Smith.*

The head brewer at 51 North Brewing is Adam Beratta. Adam brings a professional depth of brewing knowledge that helped get 51 North off to a great start. Adam started out as an avid home brewer prior to his first professional brewing job. His professional brewing apprenticeship started at Redwood Brewery in Flint in 2008. At Redwood, he learned from the award-winning brewers of Bill Wambly and Konrad Conner. Adam then became the head brewer at Great Baraboo Brewing Company in Clinton Township, where he helped turn its beer program into a well-run system. When Don was working to open the brewery, he recruited Adam to be his head brewer. At 51 North Brewing, Adam has been able to be part of the design and operation of a brewery from the launch.

Adam Beratta received a silver medal at the Great American Beer Festival in 2012. It helped to confirm what many people already knew: Adam is one talented brewer. The standard beers that 51 North Brewing Company offers are Lake Orion Light, Paint Creek Tangerine Wheat, Wind Walker Brown, Topped Out Pale Ale, Dogway IPA and Velvet Moose Chocolate Oatmeal Stout. It also offers plenty of seasonal beers, mead and wine.

Mary Gindhart, Don's wife, runs the food program at 51 North Brewing Company. She takes a made-from-scratch approach to cooking and offers a menu free of fried foods. She offers a variety of simple and approachable food items at the brewery. Customers can order everything from pot stickers and shrimp to pita pizza, burgers and salads. She features tacos on Tuesdays, brats on Wednesdays and pulled pork on Thursdays. Food is no afterthought at 51 North Brewing Company.

With the brewery being close to the Paint Creek rail trail, the brewery attracts a lot of beer and bicycle enthusiasts. Each Sunday, 51 North runs a special promotion called Sunday Fun Day. It offers one dollar off pints to all bicyclists who ride over during business hours. In the summer months, 51 North offers great outdoor seating. There is no better way to enjoy a satisfying beer after, during or before a bike ride than by sitting outside.

51 North Brewing is worth the drive up to the far north side of Metro Detroit. Add it to your local beercation and enjoy what Don, Mary and Adam have been brewing and cooking up for you in Lake Orion.

TILTED AXIS BREWING COMPANY
(303 WEST NEPESSING STREET, LAPEER)

Tom Hansen opened Tilted Axis Brewing Company in the fall of 2015. Tilted Axis is the first brewery to open in downtown Lapeer, and Doug Beedy is the brew master. Doug brings years of professional brewing experience to the company. Doug formerly brewed at Fort Street Brewery in Lincoln Park, but he has also had his hand in nearly a dozen brewhouses in Michigan during his brewing career. The company has several standard beer selections, as well as hard cider and mead. The menu finds a selection of appetizers, sandwiches and sausages, as well as a cinnamon bun option for dessert. The company name, Tilted Axis, is actually a reference to the earth's axial tilt, which is responsible for our four seasons. Tilted Axis Brewing Company has trivia nights every Tuesday and Bend & Brew (yoga) on Sundays in November. Watch the event section of its website for other interesting events.

Westside and Northwest Side of Metro Detroit

In the late 1990s and early 2000s, a handful of breweries came and went on the west and northwest side of Metropolitan Detroit. Local Color Brewing Company opened in 1997 in Novi and lasted until 2004. Fire Academy Brewery & Grill in Westland was in business from 1997 to 2000. The Matt Prentice Group of restaurants opened two different brewpubs, Bonfire Bistro & Brewery in Northville and Etoufee in Southfield; neither location made it past 2007. Copper Canyon Brewery was in business from 1999 to 2013. CJ's Brewing Company is located in Commerce Township and has outlasted them all. It opened in 1997 and is still going strong today. Until recently, craft beer lovers on the west and northwest end of town had no brewery and were left to venture out of their local communities to enjoy a handcrafted beer. That all started to change in 2008 with the opening of Liberty Street Brewing Company in Plymouth. It had the westside to itself until the latest wave of breweries finally started to open beginning in 2011 with Witch's Hat Brewing Company in South Lyon. In 2012, Northville Winery opened up a taproom to sell wine and hard cider and has now expanded to include beer. From 2014 to 2015, ten breweries have opened up on the west and northwest end of Metropolitan Detroit. Here's the story of how the west and northwest area has come alive with breweries.

LIBERTY STREET BREWING COMPANY
(149 WEST LIBERTY STREET, PLYMOUTH)

Liberty Street Brewing Company opened in the fall of 2008 and is located in the historic Old Village area of Plymouth. While Joe Walters and Mark McAlpine are the principal partners of the brewery, three other partners also joined them in the brewery operation; Jim Satterfield became the lead brewer. Joe Walters and Jim Satterfield met as members of the Ann Arbor Brewers Guild, where they both shared a love of brewing beer and an interest in starting their own brewery.

The building that houses the Liberty Street Brewing Company's tasting room was built in the 1890s. It once housed a meat market, an antique shop and, most recently, a martini bar. The taproom's bar is a woodworker's dream bar in which the former martini bar owners had invested some serious money. The brewhouse building is directly to the right when you walk into Liberty Street Brewing Company. It was added during the brewery's original construction when the building next door was demolished and rebuilt to contain the brewhouse. Above the brewhouse is an upper-level second bar and seating area for up to sixty-five people. The Upper Hall, as it is called, is used during the weekends and for private and special events. During the peak season, the Upper Hall is booked two to three nights a week. It has separate restroom facilities, a small service bar and a sound and video system to use for presentations.

Liberty Street Brewing Company uses a six-barrel system that averages six hundred barrels of production per year. It maintains six standard beers and two to three rotating seasonal selections. Liberty Street Brewing is also a licensed winery and offers house wines, hard ciders and mead. The brewery's standard beers include Steamy Windows California Common, Starkweather Stout, Red Glare Amber Ale, Liberty One Porter, Liberty Belle Blonde Ale and the American IPA. It also offers a great variety of seasonal beers including Clementine Lemon-Thyme Ale, Punkin Pie Ale, Pooh Bear Honey Porter and Majesty Bourbon Barrel Aged Russian Imperial Stout. Annually, Liberty Street Brewing Company offers a special IPA called Barber's Garden. It is made with hops grown in the hop garden behind the brewery and next to the Yer Grampa's Moustache Barber Shop. Originally, the hops had been growing behind the barbershop for years. However, today Jim helps maintain that hop garden, and Jim also has his own hop garden at his home in Livonia. The brewery uses the hops harvested from behind the shop, Jim's home and sometimes even from what customers have brought and harvested on their own. Liberty Street's customers are the true winners by getting to enjoy fresh hopped beers.

Today, Liberty Street Brewing bottles and sells draft beer in the local market. The company originally brewed its bottled and draft beers at MillKing It Productions in Royal Oak. There was an alternating proprietorship arrangement, which is an arrangement where two or more people take turns using the physical premises of a brewery. Generally, the proprietor of an existing brewery, the "host brewery," agrees to rent space and equipment to a new "tenant brewer." Alternating brewery proprietorships allow existing breweries to use its excess capacity, which in turn gives new entrants to the beer business an opportunity to begin on a small scale without investing in premises and equipment immediately. It was a great way for Liberty Street Brewing Company to test the waters of distributing its beer in the marketplace. Seeing success with its products, Liberty Street decided that it needed its own production brewery and thus opened its production-only facility in 2015. It is located in Livonia about five minutes from the Plymouth brewery. Liberty Street Brewing installed a fifteen-barrel brewhouse and

Jim Satterfield, brewer at Liberty Street Brewing Company in Plymouth. *Photo by Stephen Johnson.*

hopes to eventually brew five thousand barrels of beer per year. Joe Walters is head brew master at the production brewery, while Jim Satterfield leads the brewing at the main taproom in Plymouth. Look for Liberty Street Brewing Company bottles and draft products at finer retailers and bars in the Metro Detroit area.

The Liberty Street Brewing Company always had the notion of having a simple taproom that serves its beer. It does not offer a regular food menu, but the company does allow outside food to be brought in by patrons. Belly Busters pizza is just down the road and will deliver its delicious pies. Liberty Street Brewing offers a $35 annual and $100 lifetime mug club membership. The mug club grants members 20 percent off all purchases in the taproom. Other taproom specials include discounted growler fills on Wednesdays and happy hour beer specials daily from 3:00 p.m. to 7:00 p.m.

Liberty Street Brewing works hard to support the local home brewing community by regularly hosting meetings and discussions at the brewery. Joe and Jim also formed the Sons of Liberty home brew club, and today that club has members in Plymouth, Livonia, Canton, Westland, Northville and beyond. It meets monthly for tastings, discussions and recipe development in the brewery's basement. Every spring and fall, the Sons of Liberty home brew club brews a special batch of beer behind the Liberty Street brewery. The brewing events are in honor of National Homebrew Day and Teach a Friend to Homebrew Day. Both events are part of the American Homebrewers Association's (AHA) national programs to highlight home brewing as a hobby and gateway to a professional career in the brewing industry. The Sons of Liberty is a local chapter of the AHA.

DEARBORN BREWING (21930 MICHIGAN AVENUE, DEARBORN)

After three years of hard work and a successful crowd-funding program that raised more than $25,000, Dearborn Brewing finally opened its doors in August 2015. Dearborn Brewing is a small microbrewery located in downtown west Dearborn. John and Sheila Rucinski are the owner/operators of the brewery, which offers an on-site twenty-five-person taproom with six to eight beers on draft. Dearborn Brewing uses a small seven-gallon brew system with three-hundred-gallon fermenters. John has been home brewing for the last fifteen years and has a solid list of beer recipes that are ready to go for the brewery upstart. Dearborn Brewing does not offer any food, but it does allow food to be brought in or delivered from local restaurants. It also offers happy hour Monday through Friday from 3:00 p.m. to 6:00 p.m., when customers get one dollar off pints. Good luck to Dearborn Brewing in its westside brewing endeavor.

Farmington Brewing Company (33336 Grand River Avenue, Farmington)

In November 2014, Jason Hendricks and Jason Schlaff opened Farmington Brewing Company. Both worked at an environmental lab and are self-proclaimed science geeks who also enjoy home brewing. About five years into home brewing, they decided to take their passion for brewing beer to Farmington and opened a small brewpub in the downtown district. Jason Schlaff enlisted the help of his dad, Gary, and the three of them started their life in the beer business. By transforming the former coffeehouse, Meantobe Café, the brewery is located in the main section of downtown, a few doors down from John Cowley's and Sons, a popular restaurant and beer bar.

Farmington Brewing Company is a fairly small establishment that fits about eighty people standing. Since Friday and Saturday evenings can be pretty crowded, customers should arrive early to ensure a spot at the bar. In the summer months, it offers some outdoor seating. The brewery typically has ten beers and a hard cider on draft. The company offers a few wine options for non-beer drinkers. Farmington Brewing does not offer any food, but customers can bring in food or have it delivered in from local restaurants. Farmington Brewing is also distributing its beers on draft in the local market. Its hours are somewhat limited, so check the website to make sure it is open when you wish stop in for a beer.

Canton Brew Works (8521 North Lilly Road, Canton)

The husband-and-wife team of Barry and Cara Boggs started out as home brewers in the Chicago area. They were active in the Chicago local home brew clubs and had entered various local home brew competitions. The duo moved back to Canton to be closer to family and saw that there was not a local brewery. Therefore, they decided to take their passion for brewing beer

Cara and Barry Boggs, owners of Canton Brew Works in Canton. *Photo by Erik Smith.*

and opened the first brewery in Canton. Canton Brew Works opened as a small microbrewery in the spring of 2015.

Canton Brew Works has a three-barrel brewhouse, with its sights set on eventually upgrading to a larger system. Barry and Cara have completed the majority of the installation and brewery design. Canton Brew Works offers six beers on draft with a constantly rotating list that varies from malty to hoppy. Like a number of other breweries, it does not offer food but permits food to be brought in or delivered. In fact, there are two food options located in the same strip mall as the brewery. Canton Brew Works offers a lifetime mug club membership for $100. The mug club includes $1 off pints, $2 off growler fills and other great promotional offers. Beer fans look forward to seeing the great beer that comes out of Canton in the coming years.

North Center Brewing Company
(410 North Center Street, Northville)

North Center Brewing Company opened its doors in the spring of 2015. It is located on the outer edge of downtown Northville and across from the Kroger Grocery Store, formerly Hiller's Market. According to a *Hometown Life* article on the brewery opening, "Owner Kevin DeGrood and his team wanted to create a look and atmosphere celebrating an ultimate craft beer experience." Currently, the brewery offers a handful of beers on draft. It has a forty-dollar-per-year mug club membership available for brewery regulars. The club provides members with 5 percent off all brewery purchases, the member's name on a bottle cap for the Michigan bottle cap wall, a North Center Brewing T-shirt and accrued points for every purchase.

North Center Brewing Company does not offer regular food selections, but on select weekends, the company does offer up special food truck options for customer convenience. Brewery management is committed to using local products, vendors and contractors where possible. In fact, even the barn wood used in the brewery came from a 130-year-old barn that was being torn down in Owosso, Michigan. The brewery offers somewhat limited hours. It is closed Monday and Tuesday and open Wednesday to Friday starting at 5:00 p.m. and Saturday and Sunday starting at noon. Since those times may change in future, consult the website for hours and upcoming events. The community of Northville can now say that it has a local brewery, and customers can look forward to seeing what North Center Brewing Company has in store for them.

Witch's Hat Brewing Company
(601 South Lafayette Street, South Lyon)

Witch's Hat Brewing Company opened to the public on the day after Christmas in 2011. The name comes from the train station in South Lyon that is shaped like a witch's hat. The husband-and-wife team of Ryan and Erin Cottongim founded the brewery after they had both been laid off during the recession. The couple put together a business plan and went for broke by starting a little brewery in a strip mall in South Lyon.

Nearly three years to the day of their original brewery opening, they moved down the road. The couple officially opened a larger brewery in South Lyon on November 15, 2014. They upgraded their space from a 1,600-square-foot brewery to an 8,000-square-foot stand-alone building. The brewery now has seating for nearly one hundred, the size of its bar space has doubled and private parking was added. They upgraded the brewhouse from a three-barrel system to a fifteen-barrel system. Witch's Hat Brewing Company is now capable of producing a lot more of its standard, seasonal and bourbon-barrel aged beers with this larger-size facility. When visiting the taproom, customers find fifteen to twenty beers on draft. The brewery also sells its beer to-go via growlers, howlers and six-pack cans. Witch's Hat also partnered with Michigan Mobile canning in 2015 to produce Train Hopper IPA in twelve-ounce cans. The cans were sold out of the brewery, and the owners hope to offer other beers in cans down the road. The brewery does not have prepared food in-house, but a local food truck is on site four days a week.

Most breweries offer a mug club, but Witch's Hat takes the mug club a step further. It has partnered with the Glass Academy in Dearborn to produce one-of-a-kind glass-blown mugs. Witch's Hat has more than 1,600 mug club members. Seven hundred unique mugs make up likely the largest collection on display of hand-blown mugs anywhere. The owners believe that it is the community support that has made Witch's Hat Brewing Company so successful. Mug club programs are a great way to get to know your customers, and Witch's Hat works hard to create that connection with its customers, as well as the overall community. Each August, Witch's Hat Brewing runs an amazing beer event at the brewery called Fury for a Feast. The 2015 event raised $6,000 for Gleaners Food Bank and Blessings in a Backpack. At the event, Witch's Hat offered live music, great food and more than a dozen bourbon barrel–aged beers on draft. It has special mug club–only limited-edition bottle releases that folks line up to purchase. Since it does not offer these beers in bottles at any other time during the year, it has become a very popular event and another great reason to join the club. Lastly, another great perk of the mug club is its loyalty program, where the loyalty card earns members 2 percent back on all purchases made in the taproom.

Witch's Hat visitors should sample Train Hopper IPA if you like something hoppy, Edwards Portly Brown Ale if you like something malty and sweet or Three Kord Kolsch if you like something light and refreshing. Depending on the season, the brewery may be offering some amazing bourbon barrel–aged beers and tasty stouts. Check its website to see what is currently on draft. In 2015, Witch's Hat produced 1,300 barrels of beer. With the added capacity of the new location and continued expansion, Witch's Hat hopes to eventually produce 5,000 barrels of beer per year.

Mug club mugs from Witch's Hat Brewing Company in South Lyon. *Photo by Erik Smith.*

If you cannot make it out to the taproom, look for its beer on draft in finer bars, restaurants and bowling alleys all over Metro Detroit. The local South Lyon community has embraced Witch's Hat Brewing Company by carrying its product on draft all over town. This even includes the local bowling alley, which has three Witch's Hat beers on tap. With that kind of endorsement, Witch's Hat Brewing Company is on the road to continued success.

THIRD MONK BREWING COMPANY
(228 SOUTH LAFAYETTE AVENUE, SOUTH LYON)

Third Monk Brewing Company opened in June 2015 and is located just down the road from Witch's Hat Brewing in South Lyon. Jim Robinson and Darlene Dunlop started Third Monk Brewing with a three-barrel brewhouse. The couple hopes to expand to a larger system over time. Although the brewery did not open with a kitchen, it does allow outside food to be brought in by customers.

A HISTORY OF BREWING IN THE MOTOR CITY

DRAUGHT HORSE BREWERY
(57221 GRAND RIVER AVENUE, LYON TOWNSHIP)

Draught Horse Brewery is the new kid in town. It opened its doors in September 2015 and is located in the former Rio Grande restaurant building. Brad Tiernan and Jason Landis founded the brewery. Brad owns two draft horses that became the inspiration for the brewery's branding, the barn-themed taproom and the merchandise. The theme fits with the brewery's country location and proximity to local rail trails. In addition to having a parking lot for vehicles, there are areas for motorcycles, bike and horse parking.

The brewpub has space for fifty patrons inside and twenty-five outside. It offers a full food menu, including a build-your-own mac-and-cheese option. Draught Horse Brewing offers ten beers on draft brewed in a 2.5-barrel brewhouse. The core beers include blonde ale, red ale, stout, pale ale and an IPA, and there are five rotating beers.

A unique feature of the brewpub is what the owners call Brew 4 U. According to the website, "Want a great tasting beer brewed exclusively for your business? Get the chance to collaborate with our brew master to create and name your restaurant's new craft beer to have on tap in your establishment." It's essentially a brewery creating a customized beer that is sold exclusively at another establishment. The brewpub has had great success with the unique Brew 4 U program.

ASCENSION BREWING COMPANY
(42000 GRAND RIVER AVENUE, NOVI)

Ascension Brewing Company opened in July 2015. It is the brainchild of owner and brewer Adam Czap, and it is Novi's first nanobrewery. It's conveniently located close to Twelve Oaks Mall and the Novi Town Center shopping areas. The brewhouse consists of a 3.5-barrel system, and Ascension Brewing Company offers twelve beers on draft or available to-go via growlers.

Ascension offers a farm-to-table menu, including sandwiches that feature bread from Ann Arbor's Zingerman's Bakehouse. Watch its website for special events and a menu of food items that changes seasonally. Now that Ascension has opened, Novi locals no longer have to drive to neighboring communities to enjoy a freshly made beer.

DETROIT BEER

CJ's Brewing Company
(8115 Richardson Road, Commerce Township)

CJ's Brewing Company was part of the first wave of brewpubs to open in the Detroit area. Founded in 1997 by Cary "CJ" Moore, it is a family-friendly brewpub with a restaurant and bar seating area that can accommodate 180 people. CJ's also offers outdoor seating in the hop garden patio. The hop vines that are growing around the patio came from Dan Scarsella's grandparents' farm. Dan was the original brewer at CJ's, and he also helped with the original breweriana décor you see throughout the brewpub. Dan was the brewer at CJ's until 2006, when JT Ross replaced him. JT has continued in Dan's shoes by making a great variety of quality and consistent beers.

CJ's brewhouse is a 7-barrel system. It recently added extra fermenters to keep up with the demand and improve production. CJ's can now produce up to 1,200 barrels annually, and it brews five standard beers and up to three seasonal beers at any time. It offers weekly cask ale tapping for all of the fans of real ale. Growlers and six-packs are available to-go at the brewpub. CJ's Brewing Company offers a very attractive mug club for its customers. The fee is thirty dollars (annual) or fifty dollars (lifetime), and members receive twenty-five-ounce pours for the sixteen-ounce price, specials on growler fills and an annual mug club appreciation party.

CJ's offers a full menu of food that is sure to satisfy a customer's hunger, including daily specials such as pizza night on Monday, burger night on Tuesday, Mexican night on Wednesday, mug club night on Thursday, fish and chips on Friday, all-day happy hour on Saturday and kids-eat-free on Sunday. CJ's offers a little something for every taste.

CJ's also has a satellite location inside the USA Hockey Arena, formerly the Compuware Arena in Plymouth. The arena is home to the USA Hockey National Team Development Program. The Plymouth CJ's location includes all of its beers and select offerings from its food menu. It also offers other breweries' beers on draft and in bottles. Growler fills of the four standard CJ's Brewing Company beers are also available for only nine dollars per fill.

Residents or visitors to the northern Oakland County community of Commerce Township or attending a USA hockey team development game in Plymouth can stop in and enjoy great beer and food at CJ's Brewing Company in Commerce Township or Plymouth.

A HISTORY OF BREWING IN THE MOTOR CITY

Brewery Becker (500 West Main Street, Brighton)

Brewery Becker opened in 2014 and has been a labor of love for the owner and brewer Matt Becker. Matt and his father, John, first started working toward opening a brewery in 2007. They scouted different locations around the northwest side of Metro Detroit and eventually found a historic building in downtown Brighton. The historic preservation and construction turned into a nearly four-year project. The building once housed the Western House Hotel. It was constructed in 1873 and helped to house people visiting Brighton via the train since the building is located right next to the tracks. Until the early 2000s, Western House provided office space on the ground level and rooms for rent on the upper floors. The Beckers chose this building because they wanted to preserve a piece of downtown Brighton's historic past and felt that it also had the space necessary to house the brewery. The Beckers have invested nearly $2 million into the multi-year renovation of the interior and exterior of the building, and they added one of the largest beer gardens in Oakland County. A visit to Brewery Becker is needed to truly appreciate the level of detail the Beckers have applied in order to bring this building back to life as a brewery.

The brewhouse consists of a seven-barrel system, and there are typically fourteen beers on tap. Matt Becker brews his beers with a heavy European influence, and the beer list changes constantly. Matt favors German, Belgian and some ancient beer styles not usually found in the Detroit area. Brewery Becker offers a mug club and a horn club. The mug club is priced at fifty dollars per year for which members get one dollar off beers and growler fills plus invitations to special beer events. The horn club gets everything the mug club does, but it also includes the member's very own hand-carved Viking-style drinking horn to keep and use when patronizing Brewery Becker. Of the more than two hundred breweries in Michigan, Brewery Becker is likely the only one offering drinking horns. Additionally, horn club members get to attend the exclusive Chain of Lakes Viking river cruise. Attendees learn about the history of the Huron River while enjoying beer and food—a pretty cool perk for being part of the exclusive horn club.

Brewery Becker has only a light food menu, but it does allow outside food to be delivered or brought into the brewery. Since only beer and soda are sold at the brewery, it also allows people to bring their own bottle of wine for a small corkage fee. The second floor and mezzanine level of Brewery Becker are available for private events. See its website for more information. On Wednesday nights, the brewery offers an open mic night for its customers'

127

pleasure. It also offers other live entertainment on select nights throughout the year. The amazing brewery building and, of course, the beer make it worth the trip.

RIVER'S EDGE BREWING COMPANY
(125 SOUTH MAIN STREET, MILFORD)

River's Edge Brewing Company opened in June 2014 and is Milford's first craft brewery. The brewery is adjacent to Milford's Central Park and the Huron River. It is decorated in an industrial motif with a slightly rustic flavor, which provides a casual feel in the sixty-seat brewery. In the summer, twenty-five outdoors seats expand the brewery's seating capacity.

According to the River's Edge website, three local families founded River's Edge Brewing Company. Tom and Mary Ouvry, Michael and Gill Last and Ryan and Carrie Wiltse were longtime friends who all live on the same dirt road. It was during one of the many nights the couples spent hanging out and enjoying some home brew that the idea of River's Edge was launched.

The owners brought in Kim Schneider as the head brewmaster. Kim had previously brewed at North Peak, Dragonmead and Bastone Breweries. She offers a wide variety of beers at River's Edge, from kolsch, wheat and saison on the lighter to mild side, Scottish and stout on the malty to bitter side and IPAs on the hoppy side. The brewery also offers wine and hard cider for the non-beer drinkers.

River's Edge Brewing Company offers a simple food menu consisting of light snacks, sandwiches and sausages. For the regulars, River's Edge Brewing offers a mug club. For sixty-five dollars per year, members drink using a .5L mug, get 20 percent off beer and food, attend a members' only annual party and receive invitations to special beer releases.

River's Edge Brewing Company has lived up to its goal of being a community-focused brewery. It offers a wide range of events including monthly yoga, regular canoe and kayak trips down the Huron River, monthly beer education and tasting and appreciation sessions. Despite being a relatively new brewery, River's Edge Brewing won a silver medal at the Great American Beer Festival in Denver in the Belgian-style Dubbel or Quadruple beer style category in September 2015. The award was for the brewery's Dubbel Entendre beer. The GABF medal is among the most sought-after awards in the brewing world and proves that River's Edge Brewing Company's beers are great.

ETERNITY BREWING COMPANY
(4060 EAST GRAND RIVER AVENUE, HOWELL)

Mike and Dayna Tran operate Eternity Brewing Company. The couple met while they were lab partners at the University of Michigan, from which they both graduated with master's degrees in mechanical engineering. Their love of craft beer led them to home brewing. Dayna eventually quit her engineering job to work as an assistant brewer with Witch's Hat Brewing in South Lyon. Mike and Dayna opened their own brewery in September 2014.

Eternity Brewing offers twelve to fourteen beer choices, as well as house-made sodas. It sells hard cider from Northville Winery and wine from Main Street Winery in Howell. Its beer choices range from blonde and wheat ales to porter and stouts to pale and hoppy. One of its specialty beers is Michigan Hopped Pale Ale, where the brewer rotates the hops used on each batch brewed and features different hops being grown in Michigan. Eternity Brewing offers gluten-free IPA, which Dayna started perfecting when she brewed at Witch's Hat Brewing in South Lyon. The company also offers Teeko Coffee Stout. This beer has a special proprietary organic blend of

Ribbon cutting at Eternity Brewing in Howell. *Photo by Erik Smith.*

coffee prepared and fresh roasted by Teeko's located right across the street from the brewery.

Eternity Brewing offers light snacks and some prepackaged food but no kitchen. It does allow customers to bring in food from local restaurants and delivery services. Since Eternity is in a strip mall, there are multiple food options just down the road. For the brewery regulars, Eternity Brewing offers a mug club program. For an annual fee of forty-five dollars, members get one dollar off eighteen-ounce mug pours, two dollars off growler pours and invitations to special beer releases and mug club–only parties. Per the Eternity Brewing website, "Only a 3.38 beers per month average or 1.875 growler fills per month to get your money's worth!" More breweries should list it out this way to show the value in mug clubs. Hats off to Eternity Brewing for thinking outside the box. Additionally, the brewery offers a variety of special activities, including a Veterans Day discount, a euchre tournament, music trivia and more. Check out the Eternity Brewing website for drink specials and upcoming events.

Block Brewing Company
(1140 South Michigan Avenue, Howell)

Block Brewing Company opened in December 2014. The owners previously ran the Shark Club Bar and Restaurant at this location. They invested more than $300,000 to remodel and reimagine this location into Block Brewing Company. Front and center is Tom Block, the head brewer and man with his name on the building. Tom has more than twenty years of brewing experience. He previously brewed for Grand River Brewing in Jackson and the former Michigan Brewing in Webberville. Tom was an instructor for a fermentation science course at Michigan State University's Artisan Distilling Program. Most recently, Tom has been part of the newly launched Schoolcraft College Brewing and Distillation Technology certificate program. The twenty-four-credit certificate program helps students learn the science of beer, brewhouse operations, marketing operations and packaging, among other skills.

Tom has designed a rotating list of twelve in-house beers at Block Brewing. The beer list ranges from light to dark and malty to hoppy beers. Block Brewing also offers other Michigan craft beer on draft and a full bar. The owners of Block purchased and installed a brand-new seven-barrel system from Quality Tank Solutions of Wisconsin during the remodel. Not only did they secure an experienced brewer and great brew system, but they also revamped their entire food program. Block Brewing Company now offers a menu consisting of in-house smoked barbecue, burgers and pizza among other things. The menu focuses on fresh meat and produce from local area farmers.

Block Brewing offers a banquet facility upstairs that can host events for twenty or more people. The advantage of hosting private events at the brewery is that it can offer food and beer, all made in-house. In the future, Block Brewing Company hopes to launch a mug club program, beer dinners, special events and, of course, plenty of beers.

As a result of the latest crop of brewery openings, it is obvious that folks on the west and northwest sides of Metro Detroit now have many more options to enjoy a house-made beer.

CLOSED BREWPUBS AND BREWERIES (AFTER 1992)

Name	Type	City	Opening Date	Closing Date
Detroit-Macinac Brewing Company*	brewery	Detroit	1993	1994
King Brewing Company	microbrewery	Pontiac	1994	2009
O'Mara's Restaurant & Brewpub*	brewpub	Berkley	1996	2001
Bo's Brewery & Bistro	brewpub	Pontiac	1996	2007
Big Buck Brewery	brewpub	Auburn Hills	1997	2006
Big Rock Chophouse	brewpub	Birmingham	1997	2013
Detroit Brew Factory	microbrewery	Eastpointe	1997	2004
Local Color Brewing Company	microbrewery	Novi	1997	2004
Fire Academy Brewery & Grill	brewpub	Westland	1997	2000
Alcatraz Brewing Company	brewpub	Auburn Hills	1998	2003

Name	Type	City	Opening Date	Closing Date
North Channel Brewing Company	brewpub	Chesterfield	1998	2000
Bonfire Bistro & Brewery	brewpub	Northville	1999	2007
Fieldstone Brewing Company	microbrewery	Rochester	1999	2002
Copper Canyon Brewery & Restaurant	brewpub	Southfield	1999	2013
Stoney Creek Brewing Company*	microbrewery	Detroit	2001	2005
Thunder Bay Brewing Company	brewpub	Auburn Hills	2003	2006
Etoufee	brewpub	Southfield	2005	2007
Malty Dog Brewery & Supplies	microbrewery	Southfield	2010	2012

*Denotes operating under new name and/or owners but at same location

Detroit / Metropolitan Detroit Current Brewery List

Washtenaw and Beyond

City	Brewery	Address	Website
Ann Arbor	Arbor Brewing Company Pub & Eatery	114 East Washington, Ann Arbor, MI, 48104	http://www.arborbrewing.com
Ann Arbor	Bier Camp	1643 South State Street, Ann Arbor, MI, 48104	http://www.bier-camp.com

City	Brewery	Address	Website
Ann Arbor	Blue Tractor BBQ & Brewery	205 East Washington Street, Ann Arbor, MI, 48104	http://www.bluetractor.net
Ann Arbor	Grizzly Peak Brewing Company	120 West Washington, Ann Arbor, MI, 48104	http://www.grizzlypeak.net
Ann Arbor	Jolly Pumpkin Artisan Ales	311 South Main Street, Ann Arbor, MI, 48104	http://www.jollypumpkin.com
Ann Arbor	Wolverine State Brewing Company	2019 West Stadium, Ann Arbor, MI, 48103	http://wolverinebeer.com
Milan	Original Gravity Brewing Company	440 County Street, Milan, MI, 49160	http://www.ogbrewing.com
Saline	Salt Springs Brewery	117 South Ann Arbor Street, Saline, MI, 48176	http://www.saltspringsbrewery.com
Saline	Stony Lake Brewing Company	447 East Michigan Avenue, Saline, MI, 48176	http://www.stonylakebrewing.com
Ypsilanti	Arbor Brewing Company Microbrewery	720 Norris Street, Ypsilanti, MI, 48198	http://www.arborbrewing.com
Ypsilanti	Unity Vibration Living Kombucha Tea	93 Ecorse Road, Ypsilanti, MI, 48198	http://www.unityvibrationkombucha.com

Downtown/DownRiver

City	Brewery	Address	Website
Detroit	Atwater Block Brewery	237 Joseph Campau, Detroit, MI, 48207	http://www.atwaterbeer.com
Detroit	Batch Brewing Company	1400 Porter Street, Detroit, MI, 48216	http://www.batchbrewingcompany.com
Detroit	Brew Detroit	1401 Abbott Street, Detroit, MI, 48216	http://www.brewdetroit.com
Detroit	Detroit Beer Company	1529 Broadway, Detroit, MI, 48226	http://www.detroitbeerco.com
Detroit	Jolly Pumpkin Pizzeria & Brewery	441 West Canfield Street, Detroit, MI, 48201	http://www.jollypumpkin.com
Detroit	Motor City Brewing Works	470 West Canfield, Detroit, MI, 48201	http://www.motorcitybeer.com
Detroit	Traffic Jam & Snug	511 West Canfield Street, Detroit, MI, 48201	http://www.trafficjamdetroit.com
Lincoln Park	Fort Street Brewery	1660 Fort Street, Lincoln Park, MI, 48146	http://www.fortstreetbrewery.com
Wyandotte	Sports Brew Pub	166 Maple, Wyandotte, MI, 48192	http://www.sportbp.com

East and Northeast Side

City	Brewery	Address	Website
Auburn Hills	Rochester Mills Production Brewery	3275 Lapeer West Road, Auburn Hills, MI, 48326	http://www.rochestermillsbeerco.com

City	Brewery	Address	Website
Birmingham	Griffin Claw Brewing Company	575 South Eton Street, Birmingham, MI, 48009	http://www.griffinclawbrewingcompany.com
Brighton	Brewery Becker	500 West Main Street, Brighton, MI, 48116	http://brewerybecker.com
Clawson	Black Lotus Brewing Company	1 East 14 Mile Road, Clawson, MI, 48017	http://www.blacklotusbeer.com
Clinton Township	Great Baraboo Brewing Company	35905 Utica Road, Clinton Township, MI, 48035	http://www.greatbaraboo.com
Commerce Township	CJ's Brewing Company	8115 Richardson Road, Commerce Township, MI, 48390	http://www.cjsbrewing.com
Dearborn	Dearborn Brewing Company	21930 Michigan Avenue, Dearborn, MI, 48124	http://dearbornbrewing.com
Farmington Hills	Farmington Brewing Company	33336 Grand River Avenue, Farmington, MI, 48336	http://fbcbrewing.com
Ferndale	B. Nektar	1511 Jarvis Street, Ferndale, MI, 48220	http://www.bnektar.com
Ferndale	Woodward Avenue Brewers	22646 Woodward Avenue, Ferndale, MI, 48220	http://www.thewabferndale.com

DETROIT BEER

City	Brewery	Address	Website
Grosse Pointe Park	Atwater in the Park	1175 Lakepointe Street, Grosse Pointe Park, MI, 48320	http://www.inthepark1175.com
Hazel Park	Cellarmen's	24310 John R Road, Hazel Park, MI, 48030	http://www.cellarmens.com
Lake Orion	51 North Brewing Company	51 North Broadway Street, Lake Orion, MI, 48362	http://www.51northbrewing.com
Lapeer	Titled Axis Brewing Company	303 West Nepessing Street, Lapeer, MI, 48446	http://www.tiltedaxis.beer
Oxford	Falling Down Beer Company	14 North Washington Street, Oxford, MI	http://www.fallingdownbeer.com
Rochester	Rochester Mills Beer Company	400 Water Street, Rochester, MI, 48308	http://www.rochestermillsbeerco.com
Royal Oak	Bastone	419 South Main Street, Royal Oak, MI, 48067	http://www.bastone.net
Royal Oak	Lily's Seafood and Brewery	410 South Washington, Royal Oak, MI, 48067	http://www.lilysseafood.com
Royal Oak	River Rouge Brewing Company	406 East Fourth Street, Royal Oak, MI, 48067	http://riverrougebrew.com
Royal Oak	ROAK	330 East Lincoln Avenue, Royal Oak, MI, 48067	http://roakbrewing.com

A HISTORY OF BREWING IN THE MOTOR CITY

B. Nektar Meadery (1511 Jarvis, Ferndale)

Brad and Kerri Dahlhofer and partner Paul Zimmerman opened B. Nektar Meadery on August 2, 2008, on National Mead Day. B. Nektar Meadery initially focused on more traditional-style meads. As the owners experimented with more nontraditional meads, they started focusing on lower-alcohol, lightly carbonated meads. The business has taken off dramatically, and today it is known nationally for its mead. B. Necktar expanded to a twenty-thousand-square-foot production facility and taproom in 2015. It has also acquired a brewery license, and it is producing beer and hard cider to complement its growing list of still and draft meads. B. Nektar Meadery is producing more than 100,000 gallons of mead annually and selling to businesses in more than twenty states. B. Necktar is truly pushing the boundaries of what mead can become as a crafted beverage.

Cellarmen's (24310 Hazel Park Road, Hazel Park)

Cellarmen's is another example of the craft beer business maturing in Metro Detroit. As brewers learn their craft and gain professional brewing experience at one brewery, they eventually leave the nest and start their own establishment. That is the case for Ian Radogost, Jason Petrocik, Dominic Calzepta and Andrew Zalewski. They all worked previously for B. Nektar Meadery in Ferndale and left to open Cellarmen's in October 2015 in the former Bolyard Lumber building in Hazel Park. This twelve-thousand-square-foot building houses the taproom and production brewery. The taproom is large and can handle nearly two hundred people and still have room for a band. Cellarmen's is producing mead, hard cider and beer. Eventually, it plans to can the mead and the cider. Canned mead would be a first in Michigan. Although there is no kitchen at Cellarmen's, food may be brought in or delivered. Cellarmen's provides a great taproom to enjoy mead and cider for local area customers.

VALENTINE DISTILLING COMPANY
(161 VESTER AVENUE FERNDALE /
985 WANDA STREET, FERNDALE)

Rifino Valentine was a day trader on Wall Street who enjoyed a good dirty martini. He dreamed of operating a micro-distillery producing vodka, gin and whiskey that would beat the big international spirit brands. Rifino has been successful in that quest. Valentine's vodka was awarded a gold medal at the prestigious San Francisco World Spirits Competition. Its Liberator Gin won a gold medal, and the Woodward Limited Whiskey won silver in the International Craft Spirits awards.

Rifino had actually started perfecting his flagship vodka at a Michigan State University distilling test facility that was housed in the former Michigan Brewing Company in Webberville, Michigan. In 2008, Valentine Distilling Company opened up a five-thousand-square-foot space distillery and lounge in Ferndale. It distills from a copper pot still that was custom-made in Germany, and the distilling process is then completed by hand. Each small batch is tasted throughout the distillation process to make sure it is just right. There are no computer-controlled systems. The Valentine distilling process is truly artisanal and handcrafted.

Although Valentine maintains the original still and lounge on Vester Avenue, in 2015 it opened a fifteen-thousand-square-foot production facility in the industrial area of Ferndale. The production-only facility helps Valentine Distilling Company satisfy the growing demand for its vodka, gin and whiskey products. The new facility will provide the needed increase in production as the company expands nationally and abroad.

MOTOR CITY GAS (325 EAST FOURTH STREET, ROYAL OAK)

Rich and Tonya Lockwood opened Motor City Gas in March 2015, giving Michigan its first dedicated whiskey distillery. Originally, Rich had been working in marketing for Compuware in Detroit, but he lost that job. He decided to turn his hobby as a distiller into a new business venture. The couple spent two years developing the business, and Rich developed distilling skills from the Michigan State University workshop program. Rich and Tonya then took over the former Vintner's Cellar space and created a rustic farmhouse-meets-urban-cocktail décor for the 2,200-square-foot distillery and tasting room. The focus is concentrated only on whiskey with everything from mashing and fermenting to distilling and aging completed in-house. Rich and Tonya are committed to providing a constant evolving variety of whiskey styles from local ingredients and crafted by local hands. Since Motor City Gas has a small distiller license and not a liquor license, it can serve only its own spirits. While the distillery does not have a kitchen, catered appetizers will eventually be served.

Two James Spirits (2445 Michigan Avenue, Detroit)

Peter Bailey and Dave Landrum opened Two James Spirits in 2013. The distillery and tasting room mark the rebirth of legal spirits production in downtown Detroit for the first time since Prohibition. Two James is currently distilling and bottling bourbon, gin and vodka. Two James is named after the two founders' fathers who were both named James. According to its website, "Two James commemorates the exceptional lives of two great men who through hard work, perseverance and passion for life, were able to leave lasting impressions on the people they loved and the communities in which they lived." The distillery is housed in a former taxicab garage. It is one of more than twenty micro-distillers in Michigan. Two James has given its spirits names, some of which have Detroit historical significance. Black Widow Bourbon is a revived 1920s recipe. The 28 Island Vodka is named after the twenty-eight islands on the Detroit River where rumrunners used to hide their contraband. Two James Spirits' tasting room is in the shadow of the historic Michigan Central Railroad Building in Corktown.

Detroit City Distillery (2462 Riopelle Street, Detroit)

In 2014, Detroit City Distillery was founded by a group of eight friends from Bath, Michigan. The distillery is located in historic Eastern Market and is housed in a former slaughterhouse and meatpacking facility. The exposed brick and steel beams that surround the long wooden bar give the space a 1930s speakeasy kind of vibe. The bar, which was actually built in 1935, was brought in from an old storefront and cleaned up just enough to maintain that old feel. The company produces and bottles gin, whiskey and vodka using only the best local ingredients that come directly from farms near the distillery. Bottles are available to-go from the tasting room, which is open six days a week to serve crafted cocktails. It opens extra early on Saturdays to accommodate the Eastern Market crowd.

Our/Detroit (2545 Bagley Street, Detroit)

Our/Detroit is a collaboration between the global spirits company Pernod Richard and three local entrepreneurs: Kate Bordine, Jeanmarie Morrish and Lynne Savino. Pernod Richard provided the startup capital, micro-distillery and the vodka recipe. The three local entrepreneurs handle the business, sales and marketing. The first "Our" was opened in Berlin, Germany. The Detroit location, which opened in 2014, is the second location. The vodka is partly distilled, blended and hand-bottled in the micro-distillery. A tasting room is also on the premises where bottles of Our/Detroit Vodka are sold in the local market.

Blake's Hard Cider Company (17985 Armada Center Road, Armada)

Blake's Orchards and Cider Mill in Armada is a Metro Detroit–area institution. Many folks in the tri-county area have been making a pilgrimage each fall to the far northern Macomb County farm since Blake's opened in 1946. In the fall of October 2013, Blake's launched Blake's Hard Cider. It opened a winery and tasting room on its main cider mill property in Armada. The hard cider business took off like a rocket, and the company is projecting $3.5 million in revenue in 2015. The company has nineteen varieties of hard cider, all made with apples from Blake's own apple orchards. Twelve hard ciders are kept on tap, and flavors are rotated seasonally. Blake's has already expanded the business by building a larger distribution center and canning facility also located on the cider mill's property. It produces four standard hard ciders in cans, bottles and draft, which are sold on site and at various retailers.

A HISTORY OF BREWING IN THE MOTOR CITY

NORTHVILLE WINERY & BREWING COMPANY
(630 OLD BASELINE ROAD, NORTHVILLE)

Northville Winery & Brewing Company opened its tasting room in June 2012. It produces hard cider, wine and beer, all of which are available to sample in the tasting room. During the warmer months, it also offers outdoor seating. Inside the tasting room, live acoustic music is featured on select evenings. It sells its hard cider and wine to-go at the tasting room and in the local retail market. Northville Winery & Brewing Company produces a wonderful variety of packaged hard ciders including Rockin' Cock (its flagship sweet hard cider), Crimson Dew (a cherry apple hard cider), Blue River (a blueberry apple hard cider) and Red Ruckus (a raspberry apple hard cider).

The Northville Winery got its beginning located across the parking lot of the historic Parameter's Northville Cider Mill (dating back to 1873). The winery opened in 1982 and was operated by Rob and Carina Nelson. In 2014, the Nelsons added a microbrewery license and started producing taproom-only beers using grapes and apples from the west side of Michigan. The couple does the pressing, fermenting and bottling of the hard cider, wine and beer on site at the cider mill. They hope to one day add a distillery to the property and make small batch spirits.

Southeast Michigan (including Detroit) has quietly emerged as a national leader in the crafted mead, hard cider and spirits market. It will be exciting to see the continued recipe innovations that emerge in the coming years.

Beer Festivals and Brewery Tours

Beer festivals have become a regular occurrence in Detroit and in surrounding communities. Every October, the Michigan Brewers Guild holds the Fall Beer Festival at Eastern Market in downtown Detroit. This two-day event draws thousands to the open-air market. The festivals that the Michigan Brewers Guild puts on have become the standard by which all other beer festivals are measured in the state. North of downtown in the city of Royal Oak, the Royal Oak Farmers' Market is the location for nearly a dozen festivals each year related to beer, wine and spirits. Many Detroit-area communities host smaller beer tasting events as a means of fundraising. All of these beer-tasting events have helped grow the community of craft beer lovers in southeast Michigan.

All major cities in the United States and abroad offer tours. Tours to attractions, museums and historical landmarks are the typical offerings. However, starting in early 2000, food and drink tourism started to pick up in popularity throughout the United States. As more people become interested in locally made products, so, too, has the desire to visit the places that grow and make things. In 2009, Motor City Brew Tours started offering guided tours to Michigan breweries. The number of customers interested in touring breweries continues to expand every year. Visit http://motorcitybrewtours.com to learn more.

As indicated in this book, there are many great breweries to explore in the Detroit area. Take the opportunity to explore all of them. Whether you visit them with a tour operator or on your own, may you come away with an appreciation of how diverse and remarkable the beer scene is in the Detroit area today.

A Bright Future for Detroit's Beer Scene

More than three hundred years ago, Detroit was born when immigrants from many countries began to settle on the western banks of what was to become the Detroit River. Along the way, they brought a variety of beer recipes and brewing customs, and by the mid-1860s, there were as many as forty small brewers in the Detroit area. By the late 1800s, the beer business was shifting away from the numerous small breweries to several larger-scale brewhouses. In the 1920s and 1930s, Prohibition and the Great Depression reduced the number of Detroit breweries to ten by 1940. In the 1970s and 1980s, Detroit's local and regional breweries (including the famous Stroh brewery) departed the scene.

These losses (along with similar problems with the auto industry) reduced city government tax revenues and, coupled with the migration of people from the city to the suburbs, social unrest due to unemployment and other factors, resulted in significant financial problems for Detroit. Things hit rock bottom during the period from 2009 to 2013 when General Motors, Chrysler and the City of Detroit itself filed for bankruptcy. The good news is that all three of these entities have survived the bankruptcies, and signs of a bright future are on the horizon as follows:

- People are moving back into Detroit.
- New small businesses are popping up throughout Detroit.
- Sales of the Big Three automakers' vehicles have been increasing.

- Blighted areas are disappearing, and new construction is underway in many areas of the city.

An important piece of the rebirth or revival in Detroit involves beer. The craft beer movement, which started in the western United States in the 1970s, has been picking up steam in the Detroit area since the 1990s, and it has resulted in the reemergence of numerous small breweries and brewpubs throughout the Metropolitan Detroit area. People who avoided the city in the past are coming to downtown and outlying Detroit areas in droves to enjoy a craft beer at a brewpub and/or to participate in bicycle, bus and walking brewery tours, as well as beer festivals.

Other cities may profess to be "a beer city," but Detroiters know that "Detroit is where it's at for beer!"

BIBLIOGRAPHY

INTERVIEWS WITH THE AUTHOR

Eric Briggeman.
Erin and Ryan Cottongim.
Carolyn Howard.
Scott Morton.
Corey Paul.
Jon Piepenbrok.
Mark Rieth.
Jim Satterfield.
Dan Scarsella.
Ray Sherwood.
David Youngman.

BOOKS

Blum, Peter. *Brewed in Detroit: Breweries and Beers since 1830*. Detroit, MI: Wayne State University Press, 1999.

Burnstein, Scott. *Motor City Mafia: A Century of Organized Crime in Detroit*. Charleston, SC: Arcadia Publishing, 2006.

Kavieff, Paul. *The Purple Gang: Organized Crime in Detroit, 1910–1945*. N.p.: Barricade Books, 2000.

BIBLIOGRAPHY

————. *The Violent Years: Prohibition and the Detroit Mobs*. N.p.: Barricade Books, 2001.

Revolinski, Kevin. *Michigan's Best Beer Guide*. N.p.: Thunder Bay Press, 2013.

Ruschmann, Paul, and Maryanne Nasiatka. *Michigan Breweries*. Mechanicsburg, PA: Stackpole Books, 2006.

ARTICLES

Craft Brewing Business. "Kuhnhenn Brewing Co. Expansion Increases Capacity." August 26, 2013.

Crain's Detroit Business. "Brewer's Can-Do Attitude Is MillKing It for All Its Worth." March 10, 2011.

————. "Motor City Gas Micro Distillery Opens Tuesday in Downtown Royal Oak." March 16, 2015.

————. "Royal Oak's Bastone Brewery Named Small Brewpub of the Year at National Festival." October 6, 2014.

————. "Stroh's Death Knell Rang in Bell's Brewery and Era of Craft Beer." February 8, 2015.

Culinary Lore. "Origin of Word 'Hooch' for Liquor." September 29, 2012.

Daily Detroit. "First Look: New Microbrewery Brooks Brewing Opens in Shelby Township." September 23, 2015.

Detroit Free Press. "Atwater, McClure's Team Up to Launch Spicy Craft Brew." June 24, 2015.

————. "Draught Horse Brewery Hopes to Open Aug. 29 in Lyon Twp." August 20, 2015.

————. "New Royal Oak Brewery: Good Beer, Less Hipster." June 29, 2015.

————. "Sip Seasonal Beers at Brew Detroit's New Tasting Room." February 12, 2015.

Detroit News. "Cheers: River Rouge Brew Co. Opens in Royal Oak." June 3, 2015.

————. "One of Detroit's Oldest Craft Beers Debuts in a Can." July 31, 2015.

Forbes. "How to Blow $9 Billion: The Fallen Stroh Family." July 21, 201.

Hometown Life. "Brewing Company Taps into Larger Location." November 12, 2014.

Hour Detroit. "Corktown Welcomes Two New Breweries." February 13, 2015.

————. "The New Brewers on the Nautical Mile." January 27, 2015.

————. "The Snug Is Still Jammin." September 18, 2014.

———. "Spirited Competition: Valentine Distilling—Ferndale-Based Valentine Distilling Still Challenging Upscale Vodka Imports." January 18, 2013.

I'm a Beer Hound. "Falling Down Beer Company Acquires Second Location in the Village of Oxford." May 21, 2015. www.imabeerhound.com.

Jackman, Michael. "The Brewer: John Linardos Artist; Proprietor, Motor City Brewing Works." *Metro Times*, June 10, 2015.

Johnson, Ginger. "12 Things You May Not Know About Prohibition." CraftBeer.com, April 2, 2014.

Metro Times. "A Brewing Renaissance Takes Shape—Detroit Beer City." July 22, 2015.

———. "Canfield Gets Craftier with Jolly Pumpkin Detroit." May 6, 2015.

Michigan Beer Guide. "Rise of Michigan Craft Beer—2014 State of the Brewing Industry Report." May–June, 2015.

MittenBrew. "Kuhnhenn Remembers the Past, Looks Toward the Future." January 2015. Mittenbrew.com.

———. "Sherwood Brewing Puts Focus on Home-Like Environment, Easy-Drinking Brews." April 2014. Mittenbrew.com.

MLive. "Detroit's Motor City Brewing Works Partners to Transform Alley into City's First 'Green Alley.'" June 10, 2009. www.mlive.com.

———. "Jolly Pumpkin Brewing Up April Opening in Detroit." March 5, 2015. www.mlive.com.

———. "Michigan's Best Brewery: From Home Brew to Dragonmead." September 21, 2013. www.mlive.com.

———. "Michigan's Best Brewery: Witch's Hat Prides Itself on Beer, Friendly Atmosphere." September 13, 2013. www.mlive.com.

Model D. "Atwater Brewery to Expand Detroit Facilities and Build New Ones in Texas and North Carolina." February 10, 2015. modeldmedia.com.

Real Detroit Weekly. "The Past, Present & Future of Brewing in Michigan." January 25, 2012.

GENERAL WEBSITES

About.com. www.germanfood.about.com.

American Home Brewers Association. www.homebrewersassociation.org.

Beer Info. www.beerinfo.com.

Brewers Association. www.brewersassociation.org.

Discuss Detroit. www.atdetroit.net/forum.

BIBLIOGRAPHY

Falstaff Beer Fan Site. www.falstaffbrewing.com.
Found Michigan. www.foundmichigan.org.
Library of Congress. www.loc.gov.
Michigan Beer Cans. www.mbcinfo.com.
Michigan Beer Guide. www.michiganbeerguide.com.
Michigan Brewers Guild. www.mibeer.com.
Mich Markers. www.michmarkers.com.
Motor City Brew Tours. motorcitybrewtours.com.
Pfeiffer Beer Tribute Page. www.pfeifferbeer.com.
Wayne State University—Virtual Motor City. http://dlxs.lib.wayne.edu.
Wikipedia. www.en.wikipedia.org.

Brewery Websites

Ascension Brewing Company. ascension.beer.
Atwater Brewery. www.atwaterbeer.com.
Atwater in the Park. www.inthepark1175.com.
B. Nektar. www.bnektar.com.
Baffin Brewing Company. www.baffinbrewing.com.
Bastone. www.bastone.net.
Batch Brewing Company. www.batchbrewingcompany.com.
Black Lotus Brewing Company. www.blacklotusbeer.com.
Block Brewing Company. blockbrewingcompany.com.
Brew Detroit. www.brewdetroit.com.
Brewery Becker. http://brewerybecker.com.
Brooks Brewing. bbrewing.com.
Canton Brew Works. www.cantonbrewworks.com.
Cellarmen's. www.cellarmens.com.
CJ's Brewing Company. www.cjsbrewing.com.
Dearborn Brewing Company. http://dearbornbrewing.com.
Detroit Beer Company. www.detroitbeerco.com.
Downey Brewing Company. www.facebook.com/DowneyBrewingCo.
Dragonmead Microbrewery. www.dragonmead.com.
Draught Horse Brewery. www.draughthorsebrewery.com.
Eternity Brewing Company. http://eternitybrewing.com.
Falling Down Beer Company. www.fallingdownbeer.com.
Farmington Brewing Company. fbcbrewing.com.
51 North Brewing Company. www.51northbrewing.com.

BIBLIOGRAPHY

Fort Street Brewery. www.fortstreetbrewery.com.

Granite City Food & Brewery. www.gcfb.com.

Great Baraboo Brewing Company. www.greatbaraboo.com.

Griffin Claw Brewing Company. www.griffinclawbrewingcompany.com.

Jolly Pumpkin Pizzeria & Brewery. www.jollypumpkin.com.

Kuhnhenn Brewing Company. www.kbrewery.com.

Liberty Street Brewing Company. www.libertystreetbrewingcompany.com.

Liberty Street Production Brewery. www.libertystreetbrewingcompany.com.

Lily's Seafood and Brewery. www.lilysseafood.com.

Motor City Brewing Works. www.motorcitybeer.com.

North Center Brewing Company. www.northcenterbrewing.com.

Northville Winery & Brewing Company. www.thenorthvillewinery.com.

Original Gravity Brewing Company. www.ogbrewing.com.

River Rouge Brewing Company. http://riverrougebrew.com.

River's Edge Brewing Company. http://riversedgebrew.com.

Roak. http://roakbrewing.com.

Rochester Mills Beer Company. www.rochestermillsbeerco.com.

Rochester Mills Production Brewery. www.rochestermillsbeerco.com.

Royal Oak Brewery. www.royaloakbrewery.com.

Salt Springs Brewery. www.saltspringsbrewery.com.

Sherwood Brewing Company. www.sherwoodbrewing.com.

Sports Brew Pub. www.sportbp.com.

Stony Lake Brewing Company. www.stonylakebrewing.com.

Tilted Axis Brewing Company. www.tiltedaxis.beer.

Traffic Jam & Snug. www.trafficjamdetroit.com.

Urbanrest Brewing Company. www.urbanrestbrewing.com.

Witch's Hat Brewing Company. witchshatbrewing.com.

Woodward Avenue Brewers. www.thewabferndale.com.

Index

INDEX

W

Z

About the Author

Stephen received his bachelor's (BA) degree in sales and marketing from Western Michigan University in Kalamazoo, Michigan, in 1996. From 1996 to 2010, he worked in various sales positions at companies in Chicago and the Detroit area. He completed his master's (MBA) degree at Walsh College in Troy, Michigan, in 2010.

Along the way, Stephen got involved in the Detroit beer scene and became a regular at local breweries and beer festivals. In the summer of 2009, Stephen and a partner launched Motor City Brew Tours, which originally focused on bus transportation of people to various Detroit breweries. The partnership ended in 2010, and Stephen became the sole owner of the business and resigned from his full-time job.

Shortly thereafter, Stephen started researching Detroit's brewery history, as well as other Detroit history such as Prohibition, automobiles and so on. In the spring of 2011, he launched Motor City Bike & Brew Tours, which specializes in taking small groups on narrated bike tours to various historic brewery sites and other historic Prohibition/automotive/ etc. sites in Detroit, followed by a visit to a brewery for beer and food.

In the last six years, the business has expanded to where Stephen (with help from his wife, Laura, and other tour guides and volunteers) provides guided bus, bike and walking tours to breweries in downtown and metropolitan Detroit, as well as other parts of Michigan. More than ten thousand people have taken his tours thus far, and there's no end in sight.

Stephen loves his job where he gets paid to talk about and drink beer while he attracts visitors to downtown Detroit. He loves being surrounded by the many creative and innovative people in Detroit's beer industry, as well as interacting with some great people who have taken his tours. His website is http://motorcitybrewtours.com.